# THE NEW
# FISH & SEAFOOD
## COOKBOOK

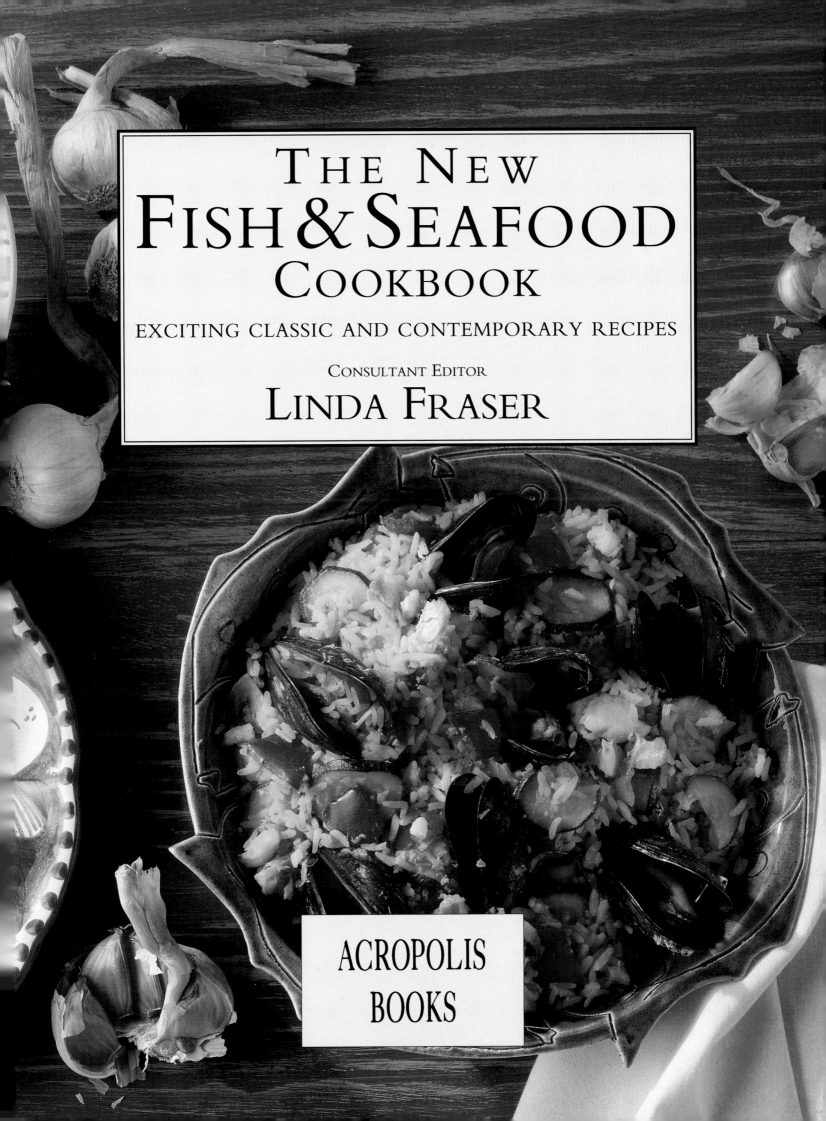

# THE NEW
# FISH & SEAFOOD
## COOKBOOK

### EXCITING CLASSIC AND CONTEMPORARY RECIPES

CONSULTANT EDITOR

## LINDA FRASER

### ACROPOLIS
### BOOKS

First published by Lorenz Books in 1995

© Anness Publishing Limited 1995

Lorenz Books is an imprint of
Anness Publishing Limited
Boundary Row Studios
1 Boundary Row
London SE1 8HP

Distributed in Australia by Reed Editions

This edition distributed in Canada by Book Express
an imprint of Raincoast Books Distribution Limited.

ISBN 1 85967 050 4

A CIP catalogue record for this book
is available from the British Library.

*Editorial Director:* Joanna Lorenz
*Series Editor:* Linda Fraser
*Designers:* Tony Paine and Roy Prescott
*Photographers:* Steve Baxter, Karl Adamson and Amanda Heywood
*Food for Photography:* Wendy Lee, Jane Stevenson and Elizabeth Wolf Cohen
*Props Stylists:* Blake Minton and Kirsty Rawlings

*Additional recipes:* Carla Capalbo and Laura Washburn

Printed and bound in Singapore

ACKNOWLEDGEMENTS
For their assistance in the publication of this book
the publishers wish to thank:

Kenwood Appliances plc
New Lane
Havant
Hants
P09 2NH

Magimix
115A High Street
Godalming, Surrey
GU7 1AQ

Prestige
Prestige House
22–26 High Street
Egham,
Surrey
TW20 9DU

Le Creuset
The Kitchenware Merchants Ltd
4 Stephenson Close
East Portway
Andover
Hampshire
SP10 3RU

MEASUREMENTS
Three sets of equivalent measurements have been provided in the recipes here, in the following order:
Metric, Imperial and American. Do not mix units of measurement within each recipe.

 The apple symbol indicates a low fat, low cholesterol recipe.

# CONTENTS

# A LOOK AT FISH

In terms of shape and structure, most fish fall into one of two general categories: round fish and flat fish.

Round fish have thicker bodies and many of their bones are attached to their fins. They can be filleted or cut into steaks or cutlets, but all will contain small pin bones.

Flat fish have a flat central bone with a row of bones attached on either side. This simple bone structure makes flat fish easy to fillet. Most are too thin to cut into steaks or cutlets.

Large fish such as tuna have a thick bone running down the centre of their bodies; spiking out from this are four rows of bones that divide the flesh into quarters. These boneless 'loins' are usually sliced into steaks.

The fat content of fish is an important consideration in deciding how to cook it. Lean fish can dry out at high temperatures, so a protective coating is a good idea when frying. When grilling, marinate or baste them. Lean and moderately lean fish are best cooked by moist methods such as steaming, poaching and baking in sauce. Oily fish, however, almost baste themselves during cooking, so they are ideal for baking, grilling and pan-frying.

Texture and flavour are also important in choosing how to prepare fish. If the flavour of the flesh is mild, it is important not to overwhelm it. But fish with rich, distinctively flavoured flesh will stand up well to spicy, pungent seasonings.

Fish that are delicate in texture need careful cooking. Pan-frying with a flour coating, steaming and gentle baking are best. However, fish with meaty, dense flesh can be cubed and put on to skewers.

## PREPARING WHOLE FISH FOR COOKING

Most fish have scales and these should be removed before cooking unless the fish is to be filleted or the skin is to be removed before serving. Fish sold by fishmongers will normally be scaled as well as cleaned (eviscerated or gutted), but you can do this yourself, if necessary. Trimming the tail gives a whole fish a neat appearance.

All fish preparation is best done in or near the sink, with cool water running. Salt your hands for a good grip on the fish.

*1* **To scale**: grasp the tail firmly and scrap off the scales using a special fish scaler or a knife, working from the tail towards the head. Rinse the fish well. Repeat on the other side.

*2* **To trim**: for flat fish to be cooked whole, use kitchen scissors to trim off the outer half of the small fin bones all round the fish.

*3* For round fish, cut the flesh on both sides of the anal and dorsal (back) fins and pull them out; the small bones attached will come out too. Trim off the other fins.

*4* If the fish is to be cooked whole, leave the fins on, or just trim them, because they help keep the shape of the fish.

*5* **To trim the tail**: if the tail is to be left on, cut a neat 'V' in the centre with scissors. The fish is now ready for cooking.

# BONING FISH

Round fish, such as trout, mackerel and salmon, are normally cleaned by slitting open the belly. It is a simple step on from here to removing the backbone. This leave a bone-free fish and a neat shape for stuffing.

When the boned fish is opened out like a book, or 'butterflied', it is approximately the same thickness throughout for even, quick cooking.

### BONING THROUGH THE BACK

An alternative boning method to the one shown here is done from the back rather than the belly. Leave the head and tail on the fish. Set the fish belly down on the work surface and use a sharp knife to slit the skin along one side of the backbone, all the way from the head to the tail. Ease the knife through the slit and work it down the side of the rib cage to detach the bones completely from the flesh. Slit the skin on the other side of the backbone and ease the knife down the rib cage to detach the flesh on that side. With scissors, snip the backbone free at head and tail ends, then lift it out along with the gills and the stomach contents.

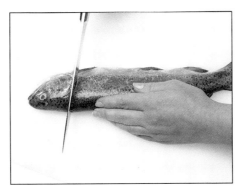

*1* If the head has not already been removed, cut it off by slicing just behind the gills. Remove the tail completely, cutting straight across.

*2* Enlarge the belly opening. Set the fish on a board, skin side up, with the belly flaps against the board. Press firmly along the backbone to loosen it. Turn the fish over.

*3* If it is possible, lift out the backbone and rib cage in one piece after freeing it with the knife. If it is necessary to cut the backbone out, slide the knife under the bones along one side of the rib cage.

*4* Gently ease the knife outwards under the rib bones, away from the backbone. Repeat on the other side.

*5* Lift up the rib cage in one piece and slide the knife under the backbone, to free it from the skin.

*6* Run your fingers over the flesh to locate any other bones and pull them out with tweezers.

*7* After boning, rinse the fish under cool running water and pat dry with kitchen paper.

# CUTTING FISH FILLETS

Fillets are boneless pieces of fish, and for this reason are very popular. A sharp filleting knife, with its thin, flexible blade, is the tool to use for removing the fillets. Be sure to keep all the bones and trimmings for making stocks.

Round fish are easy to fillet and they produce a boneless piece from each side. Large flat fish are also easy to deal with, although they are filleted slightly differently from round fish and they yield four narrow fillets – two from each side.

---

### FILLETING SMALL FLAT FISH

You can take two fillets from smaller flat fish (one from each side): Cut behind the head and down the sides of the fish as above, but do not make the central cut. Starting from the head end on one side and working down the fish, cut the flesh away from the rib bones until you reach the centre (the backbone). Rotate the fish and repeat on the other side to cut away the whole fillet. Turn the fish over and repeat to cut away the second whole fillet.

---

*1* **To fillet a round fish**: lay the fish flat, on its side. First cut off the head. With the tip of the knife, cut through the skin all along the length of the backbone.

*2* Working from head to tail and holding the knife almost parallel to the fish, use short strokes to cut one fillet off the rib bones in one piece. Follow the slit cut along the backbone.

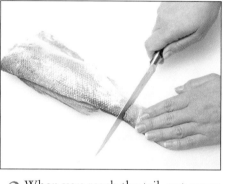

*3* When you reach the tail, cut across to release the fillet. Repeat the procedure on the other side to remove the other fillet.

*4* Run your fingers over the flesh side of each fillet to locate any stray bones. Pull them out with tweezers.

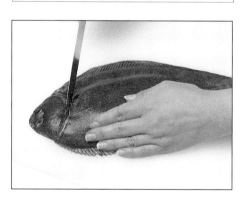

*5* **To fillet a flat fish**: lay the fish flat and make a curved cut behind the head, cutting down to but not through the backbone. With the tip of the knife, slit the skin down both sides of the fish where the fin bones meet the rib bones, 'outlining' the fillets, and slit across the tail.

*6* Slit straight down the centre line of the fish, from head to tail, cutting down to the backbone. Working from the centre at the head end, cut one fillet neatly away from the rib bones on one side. Hold the knife blade almost parallel to the fish and use short strokes.

*7* Rotate the fish and cut away the second fillet. Turn the fish over and repeat to remove the two fillets on the other side. Pull out any stray bones with tweezers.

# SKINNING FISH FILLETS

Before cooking, dark or tough skin is usually removed from fish fillets. However, if they are to be grilled, the skin helps keep the shape and should not be removed.

---

### GETTING A GRIP ON FISH

If you salt your fingers, you will get a better grip on the tail end so you can hold the skin taut as you cut. This is also a good way to hang on to fish while scaling.

---

*1* Lay the fillet flat, skin side down, tail end towards you. Make a small crossways cut through the flesh down to the skin at the tail end.

*2* Grip the bit of skin firmly and insert the knife blade so it is almost parallel to the skin, then cut the fillet away. Use a gentle sawing motion and make one continuous cut.

# CUTTING FISH STEAKS AND CUTLETS

Round fish and large flat fish such as halibut are often cut into steaks and cutlets for cooking. Steaks are cut from the tail end of the fish, while cutlets are cut from the centre. They are usually about 1–1½ in (2.4–4cm) thick.

*1* With a large, sharp knife, slice the fish across, at a right angle to the backbone, into thick slices.

*2* If necessary, cut through the backbone with kitchen scissors or a knife with a serrated blade.

# TESTING TO DETERMINE WHEN FISH IS COOKED

All seafood cooks quickly. If overcooked it becomes dry and loses its succulent quality. In the case of meaty fish such as tuna and swordfish, it can be unpleasantly chewy. It is therefore worth knowing how to judge when fish is perfectly cooked.

The flesh of raw fish and crustaceans is translucent; it becomes opaque when it is cooked.

*1* To determine whether a fish is cooked, make a small slit in the thickest part. Lift with the knife to look into the opening.

*2* The fish is ready when still very slightly translucent in the centre or near the bone (it will continue to cook when removed from the heat.

# PREPARING MUSSELS AND CLAMS

Molluscs such as mussels and clams should be eaten very fresh and must be alive when you buy them and cook them (unless they have been shelled and frozen). You can tell that they are alive if their shells are tightly closed; any shells that are open should close promptly when tapped. Any dead mussels or clams, or any with broken shells, should be discarded.

If you have collected clams yourself, let them stand in a bucket of sea water for several hours, changing the water once or twice. (Do not use fresh water because it will kill the molluscs.) Add a handful or two of cornmeal or flour to the water to help clean the clams' stomach. Clams bought from the fishmonger will already have been purged of sand.

### SAILOR'S MUSSELS

Prepare 4 litres/7 pints live mussels. Steam with 300ml/½ pint dry white wine or fish or chicken stock, 1 small chopped onion, 1–2 crushed garlic cloves and 25g/¾oz chopped fresh parsley. With a slotted spoon, transfer the opened mussels to large bowls. Add 45g/1½oz butter to the cooking liquid and stir until melted, then add pepper. Pour over the mussels. *Serves 4.*

1 Scrub the shells of mussels or clams with a stiff brush and rinse well, either in a large bowl, or under cool running water.

3 **To steam**: put a little dry white wine or water in a large pot, with flavourings as the recipe specifies. Add the mussels or clams, cover tightly and bring to the boil. Steam for 5–10 minutes or until the shells open, shaking the pot occasionally.

5 **To open a live clam**: hold it firmly in one hand, with the hinge of your palm. Insert the side of a clam or oyster knife blade between the shell halves and work it round to cut through the hinge muscle.

2 Before cooking mussels, scrape off any barnacles, then pull off their 'beards' with the help of a small knife. Rinse the mussels well.

4 Serve the mussels or clams in their shells, or shell them before using. Strain the cooking liquid (which will include all the delicious liquor from the shells) and spoon it over the mussels or clams, or use it as the basis for a sauce.

6 Open the shell and cut the clam free of the shell. Do this over a bowl in order to catch all the liquid from the shell.

# PREPARING AND DEVEINING PRAWNS

Prawns can be cooked in their shells, but more often they are peeled first (the shells can be used to make an aromatic stock). The intestinal vein that runs down the back is removed from large prawns mainly because of its appearance, although the vein may contain grit which make it unpleasant to eat.

Prawns in shell are sold with their heads. These are easily pulled off, and will enhance the flavour of stock make with the shells.

*1* Holding the prawn firmly in one hand, pull off the legs with the fingers of the other hand.

*2* Peel the shell away from the body. When you reach the tail, hold the body and pull away the tail; the shell will come off with it. Or, you can leave the tail on the prawn and just remove the body shell.

*3* Make a shallow cut down the centre of the curved back of the prawn. Pull out the black vein with a cocktail stick or your fingers.

*4* **To butterfly prawns**: cut along the deveining slit to split open the prawn, without cutting all the way through. Open up the prawn flat.

*5* **To devein prawns in the shell**: insert a cocktail stick crossways in several places along the back where the shell overlaps to lift out the vein.

# MAKING FISH STOCK

Fish stock is much quicker to make than meat or poultry stock. Ask your fishmonger for heads, bones and trimmings from white flesh.

MAKES ABOUT 1 LITRE (2 PINTS)

700g/1½lb (heads, bones and trimmings from white fish
1 onion, sliced
2 celery stalks with leaves, chopped
1 carrot, sliced
½ lemon, sliced (optional)
1 bay leaf
a few fresh parsley sprigs
6 black peppercorns
1.35 litres/2¼ pints water
150ml/¼ pint dry white wine

*1* Rinse the fish heads, bones and trimmings well under cold running water. Put in a stockpot with the vegetables, lemon, if using, the herbs, peppercorns, water and wine. Bring to the boil, skimming the surface frequently, then reduce the heat and simmer for 25 minutes.

*2* Strain the stock without pressing down on the ingredients in the sieve. If not using immediately, leave to cool and then refrigerate. Fish stock should be used within 2 days, or it can be frozen for up to 3 months.

# SOUPS & STARTERS

*Fish and seafood make delightful first courses, especially if you are serving a meaty or rich main course. For an informal or family supper, opt for a simple uncooked dish such as Smoked Mackerel and Apple Dip, or Smoked Trout with Cucumber Salad. If the weather is chilly, go for a chunky soup such as Haddock and Broccoli Chowder. For a special occasion you might like to choose Gravadlax Trout.*

# Gravadlax Trout

Although traditionally done with whole salmon, this marinating treatment also does wonders with small trout, but generally the larger the better. If you ever get locally caught, large lake trout, this is the best thing to do with them.

### INGREDIENTS

*Serves 4*
2 large trout, gutted and heads
   removed
1 bunch of dill

**Marinade ingredients for each**
**450g/1lb of fish**
7.5ml/½ tbsp coarse salt
7.5ml/½ tbsp caster sugar
7.5ml/½ tbsp crushed peppercorns

**For the mustard sauce**
5ml/1 tsp strong mustard
15ml/1 tbsp chopped fresh dill
10ml/2 tsp caster sugar
5ml/1 tsp cider vinegar
75ml/5 tbsp soured cream

*1* Slit the trout from the stomach to the tail in a straight line, then lay each fish on its stomach, opened out, and press firmly along the backbone, down to the tail. Turn over and gently, with the point of a knife, ease out the whole of the backbone in one piece, then pick out any other loose bones.

*2* Weigh the fish now and calculate the quantities of marinade seasonings. Lay one fish skin side down in a tight-fitting, non-metallic dish. Wash and dry the dill and place on top.

*3* Mix the marinade seasonings together and sprinkle evenly over the dill. Top with the other fish, cover with foil or a dish and place weights evenly on top of the fish.

*4* Chill the fish for 48 hours. Turn every 6–12 hours, basting with the marinating liquid.

*5* Mix all the sauce ingredients together and chill. Scrape away the dill and peppers from the fish and pat dry. Cut into fillets, or thinly slice the fish horizontally. Serve with hot bread and the mustard sauce.

# Smoked Trout with Cucumber Salad

Smoked trout provides an easy first course. Serve it at room temperature for the best flavour.

### INGREDIENTS

*Serves 4*
1 large cucumber
60ml / 4 tbsp crème fraîche or Greek-
  style yogurt
15ml / 1 tbsp chopped fresh dill
4 smoked trout fillets
salt and black pepper
dill sprigs, to garnish
crusty wholemeal bread, to serve

*1* Peel the cucumber, cut in half lengthways and scoop out the seeds using a teaspoon. Cut into tiny dice.

*2* Put the cucumber in a colander set over a plate and sprinkle with salt. Leave to drain for at least 1 hour to draw out the excess moisture.

*3* Rinse the cucumber well, then pat dry on kitchen paper. Transfer the diced cucumber to a bowl and stir in the crème fraîche or yogurt, chopped dill and some freshly ground pepper. Chill the cucumber salad for about 30 minutes.

*4* Arrange the trout fillets on individual plates. Spoon the cucumber and dill salad on to four serving plates. Garnish with dill sprigs and serve with crusty wholemeal bread.

# Haddock and Broccoli Chowder

A warming main-meal soup for hearty appetites.

### INGREDIENTS 🍎

*Serves 4*

4 spring onions, sliced
450g/1lb new potatoes, diced
300ml/½ pint/1¼ cups fish stock or
  water
300ml/½ pint/1¼ cups skimmed milk
1 bay leaf
225g/8oz/2 cups broccoli florets, sliced
450g/1lb smoked haddock fillets,
  skinned
198g/7oz can sweetcorn, drained
black pepper
chopped spring onions, to garnish

*1* Place the spring onions and potatoes in a large saucepan and add the stock, milk, and bay leaf. Bring the soup to the boil, then cover the pan and simmer for 10 minutes.

*2* Add the broccoli to the pan. Cut the fish into bite-sized chunks and add to the pan with the sweetcorn.

*3* Season the soup well with black pepper, then cover the pan and simmer for 5 minutes more, or until the fish is cooked through. Remove the bay leaf and scatter over the spring onions. Serve hot, with crusty bread.

---
COOK'S TIP

When new potatoes are not available, old ones can be used, but choose a waxy variety that will not disintegrate.

---

---
VARIATIONS

Smoked cod fillets would be equally good in this chowder, or, if you prefer substitute white cod or haddock fillets for half or all of the smoked fish.

---

# Prawn and Sweetcorn Soup

## INGREDIENTS

*Serves 4*

30ml/2 tbsp olive oil
1 onion, finely chopped
50g/2oz/4 tbsp butter or margarine
25g/1oz/¼ cup plain flour
750ml/1¼ pints/3 cups fish or chicken
  stock, or clam juice
250ml/8fl oz/1 cup milk
225g/8oz cooked, peeled prawns
350g/12oz sweetcorn (fresh, frozen
  or canned)
2.5ml/½ tsp finely chopped fresh dill
  or thyme
Tabasco sauce
120ml/4fl oz/½ cup single cream
salt
fresh dill sprigs, to garnish

*1* Heat the olive oil in a large heavy-based saucepan. Add the onion to the pan and cook over a low heat for 8–10 minutes, until softened.

*2* Meanwhile, melt the butter or margarine in a separate saucepan. Add the flour and stir until thoroughly blended. Cook over a low heat for 1–2 minutes, then pour in the stock and milk and stir to blend. Bring to the boil over a medium heat and cook for 5–8 minutes, stirring frequently.

*3* Chop the prawns and add to the onion with the sweetcorn and chopped fresh dill or thyme. Cook for 2–3 minutes over a low heat, stirring occasionally, then set aside.

*4* Add the sauce to the prawn and sweetcorn mixture and mix well. Remove 600ml/1 pint/2½ cups of the soup and pureé in a blender or food processor. Stir into the rest of the soup in the pan. Season with salt.

*5* Add Tabasco sauce to taste, then add the cream and stir to blend. Heat the soup almost to boiling point, stirring frequently. Serve hot garnished with dill sprigs.

# Smoked Mackerel and Apple Dip

Serve this quick, fishy dip with tasty, curried dippers.

## INGREDIENTS

*Serves 6–8*
350g/12oz smoked mackerel, skinned
   and boned
1 soft eating apple, peeled, cored and
   cut into chunks
150ml/¼ pint/⅔ cup fromage frais
pinch paprika or curry powder
salt and black pepper
apple slices, to garnish

**For the curried dippers**
4 slices white bread, crusts removed
25g/1oz/2 tbsp butter, softened
5ml/1 tsp curry paste

*1* Place the smoked mackerel in a food processor with the apple, fromage frais and seasonings.

*2* Blend for about 2 minutes or until the mixture is really smooth. Check the seasoning, then transfer to a small serving dish and chill.

*3* Preheat the oven to 200°C/400°F/ Gas 6. To make the curried dippers, place the bread on a baking sheet. Blend the butter and curry paste thoroughly, then spread over the bread.

*4* Cook the bread in the oven for about 10 minutes, or until crisp and golden. Cut into fingers and serve, while still warm, with the mackerel dip, garnished with the apple slices.

> ——— COOK'S TIP ———
> Instead of using plain sliced bread, try other breads for the dippers – Italian ciabatta, rye, or pitta breads would be excellent.

# Salmon Rillettes

## INGREDIENTS

*Serves 6*

350g / 12oz salmon fillets
175g / 6oz / ¾ cup butter, softened
1 celery stick, finely chopped
1 leek, white part only, finely chopped
1 bay leaf
150ml / ¼ pint/ ⅔ cup dry white wine
115g / 4oz smoked salmon trimmings
generous pinch of ground mace
60ml / 4 tbsp fromage frais
salt and black pepper
salad leaves, to serve

*1* Lightly season the salmon. Melt 25g / 1oz / 2 tbsp of the butter in a medium sauté pan. Add the celery and leek and cook for about 5 minutes. Add the salmon and bay leaf and pour over the wine. Cover and cook for about 15 minutes until the fish is tender.

*2* Strain the cooking liquid into a pan and boil until reduced to 30ml/2 tbsp. Cool. Meanwhile, melt 50g/2oz/4 tbsp of the remaining butter and gently cook the smoked salmon until it turns pale pink. Leave to cool.

*3* Remove the skin and any bones from the salmon fillets. Flake the flesh into a bowl and add the reduced, cooled cooking liquid.

*4* Beat in the remaining butter, the mace and fromage frais. Break up the smoked salmon trimmings and fold into the mixture with the pan juices. Taste and adjust the seasoning.

*5* Spoon the salmon mixture into a dish or terrine and smooth the top level. Cover and chill for up to 2 days.

*6* To serve the salmon rillettes, shape the mixture into oval quenelles using two dessertspoons and arrange on individual plates with the salad leaves. Accompany with brown bread or oatcakes, if you like.

# Beetroot and Herring Salad

This colourful salad uses fresh beetroot – too often underrated.

### INGREDIENTS

*Serves 4–6*
350g/12oz cooked beetroot, skinned
   and thickly sliced
30ml/2 tbsp vinaigrette dressing
4 rollmop herrings, drained
350g/12oz cooked waxy salad
   potatoes, thickly sliced
½ small red onion, thinly sliced and
separated into rings
150ml/¼ pint/⅔ cup soured cream
30ml/2 tbsp snipped fresh chives
dark rye bread, to serve

*1* Mix the sliced beetroot with the vinaigrette dressing. Arrange the herrings on individual plates with the beetroot, potatoes and onion rings.

*2* Add a generous spoonful of the soured cream to each serving and sprinkle with snipped chives. Serve with dark rye bread.

---

# Garlic Prawns in Filo Tartlets

### INGREDIENTS

*Serves 4*
**For the tartlets**
50g/2oz/4 tbsp butter, melted
2–3 large sheets filo pastry

**For the filling**
115g/4oz/½ cup butter
2–3 garlic cloves, crushed
1 red chilli, seeded and chopped
350g/12oz cooked, peeled king
   prawns
30ml/2 tbsp chopped fresh parsley
   or snipped fresh chives
salt and black pepper

*1* Preheat the oven to 200°C/400°F/ Gas 6. Brush four individual 7.5cm/3in flan tins with melted butter.

*2* Cut the filo pastry into twelve 10cm/4in squares and brush with the melted butter.

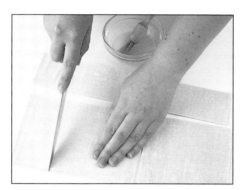

*3* Place three squares inside each tin, overlapping them at slight angles and carefully frilling the edges and points while forming a good hollow in each centre. Bake for 10–15 minutes, until crisp and golden. Cool slightly and remove from the tins.

*4* Meanwhile, make the filling. Melt the butter in a large frying pan, then add the garlic, chilli and prawns and fry quickly for 1–2 minutes to warm through. Stir in the parsley or chives and season with salt and pepper.

*5* Spoon the prawn filling into the tartlets and serve at once.

---
      COOK'S TIP
---
Use fresh filo pastry, rather than frozen, then simply freeze any leftover sheets.

# Italian Fish Soup

## INGREDIENTS

### Serves 4

30ml/2 tbsp olive oil
1 onion, thinly sliced
a few saffron threads
5ml/1 tsp dried thyme
large pinch of cayenne pepper
2 garlic cloves, finely chopped
2 x 400g/14 oz cans peeled tomatoes,
    drained and chopped
175ml/6fl oz/¾ cup dry white wine
1.85 litres/3¼ pints/8 cups fish stock
350g/12oz white, skinless fish fillets,
    cut into pieces
450g/1lb monkfish, membrane
    removed, cut into pieces
450g/1lb mussels in the shell,
    thoroughly scrubbed
225g/8oz small squid, cleaned and cut
    into rings
30ml/2 tbsp chopped fresh parsley
salt and black pepper
thickly sliced bread, to serve

*1* Heat the oil in a large, heavy-based saucepan. Add the onion, saffron, thyme, cayenne pepper and salt, to taste. Stir well and cook over a low heat for 8–10 minutes, until soft. Add the garlic and cook for 1 minute.

*2* Stir in the tomatoes, wine and fish stock. Bring to the boil and boil for 1 minute, then reduce the heat and simmer gently for 15 minutes.

*3* Add the fish fillet and monkfish pieces to the pan and simmer gently for a further 3 minutes.

*4* Add the mussels and squid and simmer for about 2 minutes, until the mussels open. Stir in the parsley and season with salt and pepper.

*5* Ladle into warmed soup bowls and serve immediately, with bread.

# Whitebait with Herb Sandwiches

Whitebait are the tiny fry of sprats or herring – add enough cayenne pepper to make them spicy hot.

## INGREDIENTS

### Serves 4

unsalted butter, for spreading
6 slices Granary bread
90ml / 6 tbsp chopped fresh mixed herbs, such as parsley, chervil and chives
450g / 1lb whitebait, defrosted if frozen
75ml / 5 tbsp plain flour
15ml / 1 tbsp chopped fresh parsley
salt and cayenne pepper
groundnut oil, for deep-frying
lemon slices, to garnish

1 Butter the bread slices. Sprinkle the herbs over three of the slices, then top with the remaining slices of bread. Remove the crusts and cut each sandwich into eight triangles. Cover with clear film and set aside.

2 Rinse the whitebait thoroughly. Drain and pat dry on kitchen paper.

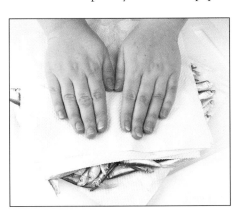

3 Put the flour, chopped parsley, salt and cayenne pepper into a large polythene bag and shake to mix. Add the whitebait and toss gently in the seasoned flour until lightly coated. Heat the oil in a deep-fat fryer to 180°C/350°F.

4 Fry the fish in batches for 2–3 minutes, until golden and crisp. Lift out of the oil and drain on kitchen paper. Keep warm in the oven until all the fish are cooked.

5 Sprinkle the whitebait with salt and more cayenne pepper, if liked, and garnish with the lemon slices. Serve at once with the sandwiches.

# Pasta with Scallops in Tomato Sauce

## INGREDIENTS

### Serves 4

450g/1lb pasta, such as fettucine or
  linguine
30ml/2 tbsp olive oil
2 garlic cloves, finely chopped
450g/1lb scallops, sliced in half
  horizontally
30ml/2 tbsp chopped fresh basil
salt and black pepper
fresh basil sprigs, to garnish

### For the sauce

30ml/2 tbsp olive oil
½ onion, finely chopped
1 garlic clove, finely chopped
salt, to taste
2 x 400g/14 oz cans peeled tomatoes

*1* To make the sauce, heat the oil in a non-stick frying pan. Add the onion, garlic and a little salt, and cook over a medium heat for about 5 minutes, until just softened, stirring occasionally.

*2* Add the tomatoes, with their juice, and crush with a fork. Bring to the boil, then reduce the heat and simmer gently for 15 minutes. Remove the pan from the heat and set aside.

*3* Bring a large pan of salted water to the boil. Add the pasta and cook until just tender to the bite, according to the instructions on the packet.

*4* Meanwhile, combine the oil and garlic in another non-stick frying pan and cook for about 30 seconds, until just sizzling. Add the scallops and 2.5ml/½ tsp salt and cook over a high heat for about 3 minutes, tossing, until the scallops are cooked through.

*5* Add the scallops to the tomato sauce. Season with salt and pepper, then stir gently and keep warm.

*6* Drain the pasta, rinse under hot water, and drain again. Add the scallop sauce and the basil and toss thoroughly. Serve immediately, garnished with fresh basil sprigs.

# Grilled Garlic Mussels

### INGREDIENTS

**Serves 4**

1.5kg / 3–3½ lb live mussels
100ml / 3½ fl oz / ½ cup dry white wine
50g / 2oz / 4 tbsp butter
2 shallots, finely chopped
2 garlic cloves, crushed
50g / 2oz / 6 tbsp dried white
  breadcrumbs
60ml / 4 tbsp chopped fresh mixed
  herbs, such as flat leaf parsley, basil
  and oregano
30ml / 2 tbsp freshly grated Parmesan
  cheese
salt and black pepper
basil leaves, to garnish

*1* Scrub the mussels well under cold running water. Remove the beards and discard any mussels that are open.

*2* Place the mussels in a large pan with the wine. Cover the pan and cook over a high heat, shaking the pan occasionally for 5–8 minutes, until the mussels have opened.

*3* Strain the mussels and reserve the cooking liquid. Discard any mussels that still remain closed.

*4* Allow the mussels to cool slightly, then remove and discard the top half of each shell, leaving the mussels on the remaining halves.

*5* Melt the butter in a pan and fry the shallots until softened. Add the garlic and cook for 1–2 minutes.

*6* Stir in the breadcrumbs and cook, stirring until lightly browned. Remove the pan from the heat and stir in the herbs. Moisten with a little of the reserved mussel liquid, then season to taste with salt and pepper.

*7* Spoon the breadcrumb mixture over the mussels in their shells and arrange on baking sheets. Sprinkle with the grated Parmesan.

*8* Cook the mussels under a hot grill in batches for about 2 minutes, until the topping is crisp and golden. Keep the cooked mussels warm in a low oven while grilling the remainder. Garnish with basil leaves and serve hot.

# Sole Goujons with Lime Mayonnaise

This simple dish can be rustled up very quickly. It makes an excellent light lunch or supper.

## INGREDIENTS

*Serves 4*

200ml / 7fl oz / 1 cup mayonnaise
1 small garlic clove, crushed
10ml / 2 tsp capers, rinsed and chopped
10ml / 2 tsp chopped gherkins
finely grated rind of ½ lime
10ml / 2 tsp lime juice
15ml / 1 tbsp chopped fresh coriander
675g / 1½lb sole fillets, skinned
2 eggs, beaten
115g / 4oz / 2 cups fresh white breadcrumbs
oil, for deep-frying
salt and black pepper
lime wedges, to serve

*1* To make the lime mayonnaise, mix together the mayonnaise, garlic, capers, gherkins, lime rind and juice and chopped coriander. Season with salt and pepper. Transfer to a serving bowl and chill until required.

*2* Cut the sole fillets into finger-length strips. Dip into the beaten egg, then into the breadcrumbs.

*3* Heat the oil in a deep-fat fryer to 180°C / 350°F. Add the fish in batches and fry until golden brown and crisp. Drain on kitchen paper.

*4* Pile the goujons on to warmed serving plates and serve with the lime wedges for squeezing over. Hand the sauce round separately.

# Spicy Fish Rösti

Serve these fish cakes crisp and hot for lunch with a green salad.

## INGREDIENTS

*Serves 4*

350g / 12oz large, firm waxy potatoes
350g / 12oz salmon or cod fillet, skinned and boned
3–4 spring onions, finely chopped
5ml / 1 tsp grated fresh root ginger
30ml / 2 tbsp chopped fresh coriander
10ml / 2 tsp lemon juice
30–45ml / 2–3 tbsp sunflower oil
salt and cayenne pepper
lemon wedges, to serve
coriander sprigs, to garnish

*1* Cook the potatoes with their skins on in a pan of boiling salted water for 10 minutes. Drain and leave to cool for a few minutes.

*2* Meanwhile, finely chop the salmon or cod fillet and put into a bowl. Stir in the chopped spring onions, grated root ginger, chopped coriander and lemon juice. Season to taste with salt and cayenne pepper.

*3* When the potatoes are cool enough to handle, peel off the skins and grate the potatoes coarsely. Gently stir the grated potato into the fish mixture.

*4* Form the fish mixture into 12 cakes, pressing the mixture together and leaving the edges slightly rough.

*5* Heat the oil in a large frying pan, and, when hot, fry the fish cakes a few at a time for 3 minutes on each side, until golden brown and crisp. Drain on kitchen paper. Serve hot with lemon wedges for squeezing over. Garnish with sprigs of coriander.

# Chilli Prawns

This delightful, spicy combination makes a lovely light main course for a casual supper. Serve with rice, noodles or freshly cooked pasta and a leafy salad.

### INGREDIENTS

*Serves 3–4*
45ml / 3 tbsp olive oil
2 shallots, chopped
2 garlic cloves, chopped
1 fresh red chilli, chopped
450g / 1lb ripe tomatoes, peeled, seeded and chopped
15ml / 1 tbsp tomato purée
1 bay leaf
1 thyme sprig
90ml / 6 tbsp dry white wine
450g / 1lb cooked, peeled large prawns
salt and black pepper
roughly torn basil leaves, to garnish

*1* Heat the oil in a pan, then add the shallots, garlic and chilli and fry until the garlic starts to brown.

*2* Add the tomatoes, tomato purée, bay leaf, thyme, wine and seasoning. Bring to the boil, then reduce the heat and cook gently for about 10 minutes, stirring occasionally, until the sauce has thickened. Discard the herbs.

*3* Stir the prawns into the sauce and heat through for a few minutes. Taste and adjust the seasoning. Scatter over the basil leaves and serve at once.

---
COOK'S TIP

For a milder flavour, remove all the seeds from the chilli.

---

# Scallops with Ginger

Scallops are at their best at this time of year. Rich and creamy, this dish is very simple to make and quite delicious.

### INGREDIENTS

*Serves 4*
8–12 shelled scallops
40g / 1½ oz / 3 tbsp butter
2.5cm / 1in piece fresh root ginger, finely chopped
1 bunch spring onions, diagonally sliced
60ml / 4 tbsp white vermouth
250ml / 8fl oz / 1 cup crème fraîche
salt and black pepper
chopped fresh parsley, to garnish

*1* Remove the tough muscle opposite the coral on each scallop. Separate the coral and cut the white part of the scallop in half horizontally.

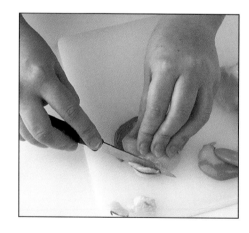

*2* Melt the butter in a frying pan. Add the scallops, including the corals, and sauté for about 2 minutes until lightly browned. Take care not to overcook the scallops as this will toughen them.

*3* Lift out the scallops with a slotted spoon and transfer to a warmed serving dish. Keep warm.

*4* Add the ginger and spring onions to the pan and stir-fry for 2 minutes. Pour in the vermouth and allow to bubble until it has almost evaporated. Stir in the crème fraîche and cook for a few minutes until the sauce has thickened. Taste and adjust the seasoning.

*5* Pour the sauce over the scallops, sprinkle with parsley and serve.

# LIGHT LUNCHES

When you are looking for simple dishes to cook, fish and seafood make excellent choices. For family meals, Parsley Fish Cakes or Hoki Balls in Tomato Sauce are easy no-nonsense fare, and in the summer kebabs made with mackerel or monkfish are an appealing way to serve fish to children. If you have friends round, treat them to spicy hot Cajun fish, or a quick and easy pasta dish such as Tagliatelle with Saffron Mussels or Spaghetti with Seafood Sauce.

# Kashmir Coconut Fish Curry

**INGREDIENTS**

*Serves 4*

30ml/2 tbsp vegetable oil
2 onions, sliced
1 green pepper, seeded and sliced
1 garlic clove, crushed
1 dried chilli, seeded and chopped
5ml/1 tsp ground coriander
5ml/1 tsp ground cumin
2.5ml/½ tsp ground turmeric
2.5ml/½ tsp hot chilli powder
2.5ml/½ tsp garam masala
15ml/1 tbsp plain flour
115g/4oz creamed coconut, chopped
675g/1½lb haddock fillet, skinned and chopped
4 tomatoes, skinned, seeded and chopped
15ml/1 tbsp lemon juice
30ml/2 tbsp ground almonds
30ml/2 tbsp double cream
fresh coriander sprigs, to garnish
naan bread and boiled rice, to serve

*1* Heat the oil in a large saucepan and add the onions, pepper and garlic. Cook for 6–7 minutes, until the onions and peppers have softened. Stir in the chopped dried chilli, all the ground spices, the chilli powder, garam masala and flour, and cook for 1 minute.

*2* Dissolve the coconut in 600ml/ 1 pint/2½ cups boiling water and stir into the spicy vegetable mixture. Bring to the boil, cover and then simmer gently for 6 minutes.

*3* Add the fish and tomatoes and cook for about 5–6 minutes, or until the fish has turned opaque. Uncover and gently stir in the lemon juice, ground almonds and cream. Season well, garnish with coriander and serve with naan bread and rice.

---
— COOK'S TIP —

Replace the haddock with any firm fleshed white fish such as cod or whiting. Stir in a few cooked, peeled prawns, if you like.

---

# Mussels with Wine and Garlic

This famous French dish is traditionally known as *moules marinières*.

**INGREDIENTS**

*Serves 4*

1.75kg/4lb (about 4 pints) fresh mussels in shells
15ml/1 tbsp oil
25g/1oz/2 tbsp butter
1 small onion or 2 shallots, finely chopped
2 garlic cloves, finely chopped
150ml/¼ pint/⅔ cup dry white wine or cider
fresh parsley sprigs
black pepper
30ml/2 tbsp chopped fresh parsley, to garnish
French bread, to serve

*1* Check that the mussels are closed. (Throw away any that are cracked or won't close when tapped.) Scrape the shells under cold running water and pull off the hairy beard attached to the hinge of the shell. Rinse well in two or three changes of water.

*2* Heat the oil and butter in a large pan, add the onions and garlic and fry for 3–4 minutes.

*3* Pour on the wine or cider and add the parsley sprigs, stir well, bring to the boil, then add the mussels. Cover and cook for about 5–7 minutes, shaking the pan once or twice until the shells open (throw away any that have not).

*4* Serve the mussels and their juices sprinkled with the chopped parsley and a few grinds of black pepper. Accompany with hot French bread.

# Omelette Arnold Bennett

After creating this dish while staying at London's Savoy Hotel, the author, Arnold Bennett, insisted that chefs around the world, wherever he stayed, cooked it for him.

### INGREDIENTS

*Serves 2*

175g/6oz smoked haddock fillet, poached and drained
50g/2oz/4 tbsp butter, diced
175ml/6fl oz/¾ cup whipping or double cream
4 eggs, separated
65g/2½oz/generous ½ cup grated mature Cheddar cheese
salt and black pepper

*1* Discard the haddock skin and any bones and flake the flesh.

*2* Melt half the butter in about 60ml/4 tbsp cream in a fairly small non-stick saucepan, then lightly stir in the fish. Cover, remove from the heat and leave the mixture to cool.

*3* Stir together the egg yolks, 15ml/ 1 tbsp of the cream and pepper, to taste, then lightly stir in the fish mixture. In a separate bowl, mix together the cheese and the remaining cream.

*4* Whisk the egg whites until stiff, then fold into the fish mixture.

*5* Heat the remaining butter in an omelette pan, add the fish mixture and cook until browned underneath. Pour over the cheese mixture, then grill until golden and bubbling.

# Parsley Fish Cakes

For extra-special fish cakes, you could use cooked fresh – or drained, canned – salmon.

### INGREDIENTS

*Serves 4*

450g/1lb cooked, mashed potatoes
450g/1lb cooked mixed white and smoked fish such as haddock or cod, flaked
25g/1oz/2 tbsp butter, diced
45ml/3 tbsp chopped fresh parsley
1 egg, separated
1 egg, beaten
about 50g/2oz/1 cup fine breadcrumbs made with one day old bread
black pepper
vegetable oil, for frying

*1* Place the potatoes in a bowl and beat in the fish, butter, parsley and egg yolk. Season with pepper.

*2* Divide the fish mixture into eight equal portions, then, with floured hands, form each into a flat cake.

*3* Beat the remaining egg white with the whole egg. Dip each fish cake in the beaten egg, then in breadcrumbs.

*4* Heat the oil in a frying pan, then fry the fish cakes for about 3–5 minutes on each side, until crisp and golden. Drain on kitchen paper and serve hot with a crisp salad.

# *Warm Salmon Salad*

Light and fresh, this salad should be served immediately, or you'll find the salad leaves will lose their bright colour and texture.

### INGREDIENTS

*Serves 4*

450g/1lb salmon fillet, skinned
30ml/2 tbsp sesame oil
grated rind of ½ orange
juice of 1 orange
5ml/1 tsp Dijon mustard
15ml/1 tbsp chopped fresh tarragon
45ml/3 tbsp groundnut oil
115g/4oz fine green beans, trimmed
175g/6oz mixed salad leaves, such as
    young spinach leaves, radicchio,
    frisée and oak leaf lettuce leaves
15ml/1 tbsp toasted sesame seeds
salt and black pepper

*1* Cut the salmon into bite-sized pieces, then make the dressing. Mix together the sesame oil, orange rind and juice, mustard, chopped tarragon and seasoning in a bowl. Set aside.

*2* Heat the groundnut oil in a frying pan. Add the salmon pieces and fry for 3–4 minutes, until lightly browned but still tender inside.

*3* While the salmon is cooking, blanch the green beans in boiling salted water for about 5–6 minutes, until tender yet crisp.

*4* Add the dressing to the salmon, toss together gently and cook for 30 seconds. Remove the pan from the heat.

*5* Arrange the salad leaves on serving plates. Drain the beans and toss over the leaves. Spoon over the salmon and cooking juices and serve immediately, sprinkled with the sesame seeds.

# Sautéed Salmon with Cucumber

Cucumber is the classic accompaniment to salmon. Here it is served hot – be careful not to overcook the cucumber.

## INGREDIENTS

*Serves 4*
450g / 1lb salmon fillet, skinned
40g / 1½ oz / 3 tbsp butter
2 spring onions, chopped
½ cucumber, seeded and cut into strips
60ml / 4 tbsp dry white wine
120ml / 4fl oz / ½ cup crème fraîche
30ml / 2 tbsp snipped fresh chives
2 tomatoes, peeled, seeded and diced
salt and black pepper

*1* Cut the salmon into about 12 thin slices, then cut across into strips.

*2* Melt the butter in a large sauté pan, add the salmon and sauté for 1–2 minutes. Remove the salmon strips using a slotted spoon.

aside.

*3* Add the spring onions to the pan and cook for 2 minutes. Stir in the cucumber and sauté for 1–2 minutes, until hot. Remove the cucumber and keep warm with the salmon.

*4* Add the wine to the pan and let it bubble until well reduced. Stir in the crème fraîche, 15ml / 1 tbsp of the chives and seasoning. Return the salmon and cucumber to the pan and warm through gently. Sprinkle over the tomatoes and remaining chives. Serve at once.

# Thai Prawn Salad

This salad has the distinctive flavour of lemon grass, the bulbous grass used widely in South-east Asia.

### INGREDIENTS

*Serves 4*

250g/9oz cooked, peeled extra large
   tiger prawns
15ml/1 tbsp oriental fish sauce
30ml/2 tbsp lime juice
7.5ml/ ½ tsp soft light brown sugar
1 small fresh red chilli, finely chopped
1 spring onion, finely chopped
1 small garlic clove, crushed
2.5cm/1in piece fresh lemon grass,
   finely chopped
30ml/2 tbsp chopped fresh coriander
45ml/3 tbsp dry white wine
8–12 Little Gem lettuce leaves, to serve
fresh coriander sprigs, to garnish

*1* Place the tiger prawns in a bowl and add all the remaining ingredients. Stir well, cover and leave to marinate in the fridge for 2–3 hours, mixing and turning the prawns occasionally.

*2* Arrange two or three of the lettuce leaves on each of four individual serving plates.

*3* Spoon the prawn salad into the lettuce leaves. Garnish with fresh coriander and serve at once.

---

COOK'S TIP

If you find raw prawns, cook them in boiling water until pink and use instead of the cooked prawns.

---

# Cajun Spiced Fish

Cajun blackened fish is a speciality of Paul Prudhomme, a chef from New Orleans. Fillets of fish are coated with an aromatic and flavourful blend of herbs and spices and pan-fried in butter.

### INGREDIENTS

*Serves 4*

5ml/1 tsp dried thyme
5ml/1 tsp dried oregano
5ml/1 tsp ground black pepper
1.25ml/ ¼ tsp cayenne pepper
10ml/2 tsp paprika
2.5ml/ ½ tsp garlic salt
4 tail end pieces of cod fillet
   (about 175g/6oz each)
75g/3oz/6 tbsp butter
½ red pepper, sliced
½ green pepper, sliced
fresh thyme, to garnish
grilled tomatoes and sweet potato
   purée, to serve

*1* Place all the herbs and spices in a bowl and mix well. Dip the fish fillets in the spice mixture until lightly coated.

*2* Heat 25g/1oz/2 tbsp of the butter in a large frying pan, add the peppers and fry for 4–5 minutes, until softened. Remove the peppers and keep warm.

*3* Add the remaining butter to the pan and heat until sizzling. Add the cod fillets and fry on a moderate heat for 3–4 minutes on each side, until browned and cooked.

*4* Transfer the fish to a warmed serving dish, surround with the peppers and garnish with thyme. Serve the spiced fish with some grilled tomatoes and sweet potato purée.

---

COOK'S TIP

This blend of herbs and spices can be used to flavour any fish steaks or fillets and could also be used to jazz up pan-fried prawns.

---

# Tagliatelle with Saffron Mussels

Mussels are served with tagliatelle in this recipe, but you can use any other pasta, as you prefer.

## INGREDIENTS

*Serves 4*

1.75 kg / 4–4½ lb live mussels
150ml / ¼ pint / ⅔ cup dry white wine
2 shallots, chopped
350g / 12oz dried tagliatelle
25g / 1oz / 2 tbsp butter
2 garlic cloves, crushed
250ml / 8fl oz / 1 cup double cream
generous pinch of saffron strands
1 egg yolk
salt and black pepper
30ml / 2 tbsp chopped fresh parsley,
  to garnish

1 Scrub the mussels well under cold running water. Remove the beards and discard any mussels that are open.

2 Place the mussels in a large pan with the wine and shallots. Cover and cook over a high heat, shaking the pan occasionally, for 5–8 minutes until the mussels have opened. Drain the mussels, reserving the liquid. Discard any that remain closed. Shell all but a few of the mussels and keep warm.

3 Bring the reserved cooking liquid to the boil, then reduce by half. Strain into a jug to remove any grit.

4 Cook the tagliatelle in a large pan of boiling salted water for about 10 minutes, until *al dente*.

5 Meanwhile, melt the butter in a pan and fry the garlic for 1 minute. Pour in the mussel liquid, cream and saffron strands. Heat gently until the sauce thickens slightly. Remove the pan from the heat and stir in the egg yolk, shelled mussels and seasoning to taste.

6 Drain the tagliatelle and transfer to warmed serving bowls. Spoon the sauce over and sprinkle with chopped parsley. Garnish with the mussels in shells and serve at once.

# Spaghetti with Seafood Sauce

The Italian name for this tomato-based sauce is *marinara*.

## INGREDIENTS

*Serves 4*

45ml/3 tbsp olive oil
1 medium onion, chopped
1 garlic clove, finely chopped
225g/8oz spaghetti
600ml/1 pint/2½ cups passata
15ml/1 tbsp tomato purée
5ml/1 tsp dried oregano
1 bay leaf
5ml/1 tsp sugar
115g/4oz/1 cup cooked, peeled
    shrimps (rinsed well if canned)
115g/4oz/1 cup cooked, peeled prawns
175g/6oz/1½ cups cooked clam or
    cockle meat (rinsed well if canned
    or bottled)
15ml/1 tbsp lemon juice
45ml/3 tbsp chopped fresh parsley
25g/1oz/2 tbsp butter
salt and black pepper
4 whole cooked prawns, to garnish

*1* Heat the oil in a pan and add the onion and garlic. Fry over a moderate heat for 6–7 minutes, until the onions have softened.

*2* Meanwhile, cook the spaghetti in a large pan of boiling salted water for 10–12 minutes until *al dente*.

*3* Stir the passata, tomato purée, oregano, bay leaf and sugar into the onions and season well. Bring to the boil, then simmer for 2–3 minutes.

*4* Add the shellfish, lemon juice and 30ml/2 tbsp of the parsley. Stir well, then cover and cook for 6–7 minutes.

*5* Meanwhile, drain the spaghetti when it is ready and add the butter to the pan. Return the drained spaghetti to the pan and toss in the butter. Season well.

*6* Divide the spaghetti among four warmed plates and top with the seafood sauce. Sprinkle with the remaining 15ml/1 tbsp parsley, garnish with whole prawns and serve immediately.

# Herrings with Walnut Stuffing

Ask the fishmonger to prepare the fish – mackerel can be used if herrings are not available.

### INGREDIENTS

*Serves 4*

25g/1oz/2 tbsp butter
1 onion, finely chopped
50g/2oz/6 tbsp white breadcrumbs
50g/2oz/½ cup shelled walnuts, toasted and chopped
finely grated rind of ½ lemon
15ml/1 tbsp lemon juice
10ml/2 tsp wholegrain mustard
45ml/3 tbsp mixed chopped fresh herbs, such as sage, thyme and parsley
4 herrings, about 275g/10oz each, without heads and tails, boned
salt and black pepper
lemon wedges and flat leaf parsley sprigs, to garnish

*1* Preheat the oven to 190°C/375°F/Gas 5. Melt the butter in a frying pan and fry the onion for about 10 minutes until golden.

*2* Stir in the breadcrumbs, chopped walnuts, lemon rind and juice, mustard and herbs. Mix together, then season with salt and pepper to taste.

*3* Open out the herring fillets and divide the stuffing among them. Fold the herrings back in half and slash the skin several times on each side.

*4* Arrange the herrings in a lightly greased shallow baking tin and bake for 20–25 minutes. Serve hot, garnished with lemon wedges and parsley sprigs.

---

# Trout with Mushroom Sauce

### INGREDIENTS

*Serves 4*

8 pink trout fillets
seasoned plain flour
75g/3oz/6 tbsp butter
1 garlic clove, chopped
10ml/2 tsp chopped fresh sage
350g/12oz mixed wild or cultivated mushrooms
90ml/6 tbsp dry white wine
250ml/8fl oz/1 cup double cream
salt and black pepper

> ——— COOK'S TIP ———
>
> Use a large sharp knife to ease the skin from the trout fillets, then pull out any bones from the flesh – a pair of tweezers makes easy work of this fiddly task!

*1* Remove the skin from the trout fillets, then carefully remove any bones.

*2* Lightly dust the trout fillets on both sides in the seasoned flour, shaking off any excess.

*3* Melt the butter in a large frying pan, add the trout fillets and fry gently over a moderate heat for 4–5 minutes, turning once. Remove from the pan and keep warm.

*4* Add the garlic, sage and mushrooms to the pan and fry until softened.

*5* Pour in the wine and boil briskly to allow the alcohol to evaporate. Stir in the cream and seasoning.

*6* Serve the trout fillets on warmed plates with the sauce spooned over. Garnish with a few fresh sage sprigs, if you have them.

# Hoki Balls in Tomato Sauce

This quick meal is a good choice for young children, as you can guarantee no bones. If you like, add a dash of chilli sauce.

### INGREDIENTS 

*Serves 4*

450g/1lb white fish fillets such as hoki or cod, skinned
60ml/4 tbsp fresh wholemeal breadcrumbs
30ml/2 tbsp snipped fresh chives or spring onions
400g/14oz can chopped tomatoes
50g/2oz/¾ cup button mushrooms, sliced
salt and black pepper

*1* Cut the fish fillets into large chunks and place in a food processor. Add the whole-wheat breadcrumbs and chives or spring onions. Season to taste with salt and pepper, and process until the fish is finely chopped, but still has some texture left.

*2* Divide the fish mixture into about 16 even-sized pieces, then mould them into balls with your hands.

*3* Place the tomatoes and mushrooms in a wide saucepan and cook over a medium heat until boiling. Add the fish balls, cover and simmer for about 10 minutes, until cooked. Serve hot.

---
VARIATION
---

Instead of using a can of chopped tomatoes and fresh mushrooms, you could substitute a jar of ready-made tomato and mushroom sauce. Just add the fish balls and simmer for 10 minutes.

---
COOK'S TIP
---

The fish balls can be prepared several hours in advance if covered and kept in the refrigerator.

# Tuna and Corn Fish Cakes

*OK*
*TRY ADDING 1 EGG*
*TO MAKE IT LESS*
*FRAGILE*
*? ADD PEPPER FLAKES ?*

These economical little tuna fish cakes are quick to make. Either use fresh mashed potatoes, or make a less fussy version with instant mashed potatoes.

## INGREDIENTS 🍎

*Serves 4*

300g/11oz/1¼ cups cooked mashed
  potatoes
200g/7oz can tuna in vegetable oil,
  drained
115g/4oz/¾ cup canned or frozen
  sweetcorn
30ml/2 tbsp chopped fresh parsley
50g/2oz/1 cup fresh white or wholemeal breadcrumbs
salt and black pepper
lemon wedges, to serve

*1* Place the mashed potato in a bowl and stir in the tuna, sweetcorn and chopped parsley.

*2* Season the mixture to taste with salt and pepper, then shape into eight patty shapes with your hands.

*3* Spread out the breadcrumbs on a plate and press the fish cakes into the breadcrumbs to coat lightly, then place on a baking sheet.

*4* Cook the fish cakes under a moderately hot grill until crisp and golden brown, turning once. Serve hot, with lemon wedges and fresh vegetables.

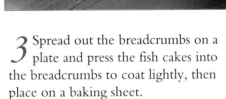

—— COOK'S TIP ——

To give the fish cakes a crisper crust, dip the fish cakes in beaten egg before coating them in the breadcrumbs, then fry in a little hot oil until golden.

—— VARIATIONS ——

For simple variations which are just as nutritious, try using canned sardines, red or pink salmon, or smoked mackerel in place of the tuna.

# Seafood Salad Provençale

You can't beat this salad for an almost instant starter or main course, and it is perfect for a buffet table as it keeps so well.

## INGREDIENTS

*Serves 4*

350g/12oz mixed cooked seafood
  (such as peeled prawns, mussels,
  winkles and crabsticks)
30ml/2 tbsp ready-made tomato sauce
1 garlic clove, crushed
60ml/4 tbsp pimiento or mixed pepper antipasti
60ml/4 tbsp artichoke antipasti
½ yellow pepper, seeded and sliced
lemon juice, to taste
30ml/2 tbsp white wine (optional)
salt and black pepper
30ml/2 tbsp chopped fresh parsley and
  whole prawns, to garnish

*1* Toss the seafood in the tomato sauce, add the garlic and leave for 5–10 minutes to absorb the flavours.

*2* Mix together the pimiento or mixed pepper antipasti with the artichoke antipasti, the yellow pepper, lemon juice and wine, if using.

*3* Stir in the seafood mixture, season to taste, and chill. Sprinkle with chopped parsley and garnish with whole prawns before serving.

# Monkfish and Potato Kebabs

Monkfish is a good, firm fish so it works well on kebabs and when cooked over a fierce heat.

## INGREDIENTS

*Serves 4*

12–16 small new potatoes, cooked
12–16 seedless grapes
10cm/4in piece cucumber, peeled and
  cut in eight pieces
275–350g/10–12oz monkfish tail,
  boned and cubed
75g/3oz/6 tbsp butter
grated rind and juice of 1 lime
5ml/1 tsp grated fresh root ginger
15ml/1 tbsp chopped fresh parsley
45–60ml/3–4 tbsp white wine
salt and black pepper

*1* Arrange the potatoes, grapes, cucumber and monkfish cubes alternately on skewers.

*2* Melt two-thirds of the butter and stir in the lime rind and juice, ginger, seasoning and half the parsley. Brush this all over the kebabs.

*3* Preheat the grill and cook the kebabs, in a dish or on a sheet of foil to catch all the juices, for 2 minutes on each side. Baste occasionally.

*4* When cooked, transfer the kebabs to hot plates while heating the juices with the wine and the remaining butter. Check the seasoning, sprinkle the kebabs with parsley and serve with a salad and the tangy lime sauce.

# Mackerel with Mustard and Lemon

Mackerel must be really fresh to be enjoyed. Look for bright, firm-looking fish.

### INGREDIENTS

*Serves 4*

4 fresh mackerel, about 275g/10oz
  each, gutted and cleaned
175–225g/6–8oz young spinach
  leaves

**For the mustard and lemon butter**

115g/4oz/½ cup butter, melted
30ml/2 tbsp wholegrain mustard
grated rind of 1 lemon
30ml/2 tbsp lemon juice
45ml/3 tbsp chopped fresh parsley
salt and black pepper

*1* To prepare each mackerel, cut off the heads just behind the gills, using a sharp knife, then cut along the belly so that the fish can be opened out flat.

*2* Place the fish on a board, skin-side up, and, with the heel of your hand, press along the backbone to loosen it.

*3* Turn the fish the right way up and pull the bone away from the flesh. Remove the tail and cut each fish in half lengthways. Wash and pat dry.

*4* Score the skin three or four times, then season the fish. To make the mustard and lemon butter, mix together the melted butter, mustard, lemon rind and juice, parsley and seasoning. Place the mackerel on a grill rack. Brush a little of the butter over the mackerel and grill for 5 minutes each side, basting occasionally, until cooked through.

*5* Arrange the spinach leaves in the centre of four large plates. Place the mackerel on top. Heat the remaining butter in a small pan until sizzling and pour over the mackerel. Serve at once.

# Mackerel Kebabs with Parsley Dressing

Oily fish such as mackerel are ideal for broiling as they cook quickly and need no extra oil.

**INGREDIENTS** 🍎

*Serves 4*
450g/1lb mackerel fillets
finely grated rind and juice of
  1 lemon
45ml/3 tbsp chopped fresh parsley
12 cherry tomatoes
8 pitted black olives
salt and black pepper

*1* Cut the fish into 4cm/1½in chunks and place in a bowl with half the lemon rind and juice, half the parsley and some seasoning. Cover the bowl and leave to marinate for 30 minutes.

*2* Thread the chunks of fish on to eight long wooden or metal skewers, alternating them with the cherry tomatoes and olives. Cook the kebabs under a hot grill for about 3–4 minutes, turning the kebabs occasionally, until the fish is cooked.

*3* Mix the remaining lemon rind and juice with the remaining parsley in a small bowl, then season to taste with salt and pepper. Spoon the dressing over the kebabs and serve hot, with plain boiled rice or noodles and a leafy green salad.

---

COOK'S TIP

When using wooden or bamboo kebab skewers, soak them first in a bowl of cold water for a few minutes to help prevent them burning.

---

VARIATIONS

Other firm fleshed fish could be used in place of the mackerel – for a special occasion you could opt for salmon fillet or monkfish tail. Or try a mixture of the two, thread the fish chunks alternately on to the skewers with the tomatoes and olives.

# Seafood Pancakes

Smoked haddock imparts a wonderful flavour to the filling.

## INGREDIENTS

*Serves 4–6*

**For the pancakes**
115g / 4oz / 1 cup plain flour
pinch of salt
1 egg, plus 1 egg yolk
300ml / ½ pint / 1¼ cups milk
15ml / 1 tbsp melted butter, plus extra
　for cooking
50–75g / 2–3oz Gruyère cheese,
　grated

**For the filling**
225g / 8oz smoked haddock fillet
225g / 8oz fresh haddock fillet
300ml / ½ pint / 1¼ cups milk
150ml / ¼ pint / ⅔ cup single cream
40g / 1½oz / 3 tbsp butter
40g / 1½oz / ¼ cup plain flour
freshly grated nutmeg
2 hard-boiled eggs, shelled and chopped
salt and black pepper
curly salad leaves, to serve

*1* To make the pancakes, sift the flour and salt into a bowl. Make a well in the centre and add the eggs. Whisk the eggs, starting to incorporate some of the flour from around the edges.

*2* Gradually add the milk, whisking all the time until the batter is smooth and the consistency of thin cream. Stir in the melted butter.

*3* Heat a small crêpe pan or omelette pan until hot, then rub round the inside of the pan with a pad of kitchen paper dipped in melted butter.

*4* Pour about 30ml/2 tbsp of the batter into the pan, then tip the pan to coat the base evenly. Cook for about 30 seconds until the underside of the pancake is brown.

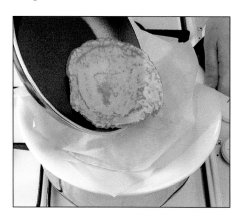

*5* Flip the pancake over and cook the other side until lightly browned. Repeat to make 12 pancakes, rubbing the pan with melted butter between each pancake. Stack the pancakes as you make them between sheets of greaseproof paper. Keep warm on a plate set over a pan of simmering water.

*6* Put the haddock fillets in a large pan. Add the milk and poach for 6–8 minutes, until just tender. Lift out the fish using a slotted spoon and, when cool enough to handle, remove the skin and any bones. Reserve the milk.

*7* Measure the cream into a jug, then strain enough of the milk into the jug to make the quantity up to 450ml/ ¾ pint/1⅞ cups.

*8* Melt the butter in a pan, stir in the flour and cook gently for 1 minute. Gradually mix in the milk mixture, stirring continuously to make a smooth sauce. Cook for 2–3 minutes, until thickened. Season with salt, pepper and nutmeg. Roughly flake the haddock and fold into the sauce with the eggs. Leave to cool.

*9* Preheat the oven to 180°C/350°F/ Gas 4. Divide the filling among the pancakes. Fold the sides of each pancake into the centre, then roll them up to enclose the filling completely.

*10* Butter four or six individual ovenproof dishes and arrange 2–3 filled pancakes in each, or butter one large dish for all the pancakes. Brush with melted butter and cook for 15 minutes. Sprinkle over the Gruyère and cook for a further 5 minutes, until warmed through. Serve hot with a few curly salad leaves.

---
COOK'S TIP
---

Add cooked, peeled prawns, smoked mussels or cooked fresh mussels removed from their shells to the filling, instead of the chopped hard-boiled egg.

# Stuffed Plaice Rolls

Plaice fillets are a good choice because they are mild in flavour, easy to cook, and free of bones. Have your fillets prepared when you buy them.

### INGREDIENTS 

*Serves 4*

2 carrots, grated
1 courgettes, grated
60ml/4 tbsp fresh wholemeal
 breadcrumbs
15ml/1 tbsp lime or lemon juice
4 plaice fillets
salt and black pepper

*1* Preheat the oven to 200°C/400°F/ Gas 6. Mix together the grated carrots and courgettes. Stir in the breadcrumbs, lime juice, and seasoning.

*2* Lay the fish fillets skin side up and divide the stuffing among them, spreading it evenly.

*3* Roll up the fillets to enclose the stuffing and place in an ovenproof dish. Cover and bake for about 30 minutes, or until the fish flakes easily. Serve hot with new potatoes.

---
COOK'S TIP
---

This recipe creates its own delicious juices, but for an extra sauce, stir chopped fresh parsley into a little low fat fromage frais and serve with the fish.

---
VARIATIONS
---

Lemon sole could be used instead of plaice. Or, for a change, buy thick pieces of cod or salmon fillet and simply top them with the carrot and courgette mixture.

# Haddock with Parsley Sauce

As the fish has to be kept warm while the sauce is made, take care not to overcook it.

## INGREDIENTS

*Serves 4*
4 haddock fillets, about 175g/
  6oz each
50g/2oz/4 tbsp butter
150ml/¼ pint/⅔ cup milk
150ml/¼ pint/⅔ cup fish stock
1 bay leaf
20ml/4 tsp plain flour
60ml/4 tbsp cream
1 egg yolk
45ml/3 tbsp chopped fresh parsley
grated rind and juice of ½ lemon
salt and black pepper

*1* Place the fish in a frying pan, add half the butter, the milk, fish stock, bay leaf and seasoning, and heat over a low-medium heat to simmering point. Lower the heat, cover the pan and poach the fish for 10–15 minutes, depending on the thickness of the fillets, until the fish is tender and the flesh just begins to flake.

*2* Transfer the fish to a warmed serving plate, cover the fish and keep warm while you make the sauce. Return the cooking liquid to the heat and bring to the boil, stirring. Simmer for about 4 minutes, then remove from the heat.

*3* Melt the remaining butter in a saucepan, stir in the flour and cook, stirring, for 1 minute. Remove from the heat and gradually stir in the fish cooking liquid. Return to the heat and bring to the boil, stirring. Simmer for about 4 minutes, stirring frequently. Discard the bay leaf.

*4* Remove the pan from the heat, blend the cream into the egg yolk, then stir into the sauce with the parsley. Reheat gently, stirring, for a few minutes; do not allow to boil.

*5* Remove from the heat and add the lemon juice and rind, and season to taste. Pour into a warmed sauceboat and serve with the fish.

# MID-WEEK SUPPERS

In the middle of the week, when you are short of time to cook, dishes made with fish or seafood are ideal – Baked Fish Creole-Style can be put together very speedily. If you have more time, fish pies, either topped with potato or filo pastry, are good. If you would like to try something a little different, opt for Moroccan Fish Tagine, Cod with Spiced Red Lentils or Spanish Seafood Paella.

# Fisherman's Casserole

## INGREDIENTS

### Serves 4–6

450g/1lb mixed firm fish fillets, such
   as cod, haddock and monkfish
50g/2oz/4 tbsp butter
1 onion, sliced
1 celery stick, sliced
350g/12oz potatoes, cut into chunks
750ml/1¼ pints/3⅔ cups fish stock
bouquet garni
150g/5oz frozen broad beans
300ml/½ pint/1¼ cups milk
115g/4oz cooked, peeled prawns
8 shelled mussels
salt and black pepper
chopped parsley, to garnish

*1* Skin the fish and cut the flesh into
bite-sized chunks using a large
sharp knife. Heat the butter in a
saucepan, then fry the onion and celery
until softened but not coloured. Stir
the chunks of potato into the pan and
cook for 1–2 minutes.

*2* Add the stock and bouquet garni.
Bring to the boil, cover and simmer for 20 minutes, until tender.

*3* Add the fish, beans and milk and
simmer for 6 minutes, or until the
fish flakes. Add the prawns, mussels
and seasoning and warm through.
Sprinkle with parsley to serve.

---

# Potato-topped Fish Pie

## INGREDIENTS

### Serves 4

400ml/14fl oz/1¾ cups milk
1 bay leaf
¼ onion, sliced
450g/1lb haddock or cod fillet
225g/8oz smoked haddock fillet
3 hard-boiled eggs, chopped
65g/2½oz/5 tbsp butter
25g/1oz/2 tbsp plain flour
115g/4oz/1 cup peas
75g/3oz prawns
30ml/2 tbsp chopped fresh parsley
lemon juice, to taste
500g/1¼lb cooked mashed potatoes
60ml/4 tbsp hot milk
60ml/4 tbsp grated Cheddar cheese
salt and black pepper

*1* Place 350ml/12fl oz/1½ cups milk,
the bay leaf and onion in a
saucepan, then add the fish. Cover and
poach for 8–10 minutes. Strain and
reserve the milk. Flake the fish into a
pie dish, discarding the skin and any
bones. Add the eggs.

*2* Melt 25g/1oz/2 tbsp of the butter
in a saucepan, stir in the flour and
cook gently for 1 minute, stirring.
Remove from the heat and stir in the
reserved milk. Return to the heat and
bring to the boil, stirring. Simmer the
sauce for 4 minutes, stirring all the
time. Remove from the heat and stir
in the peas and prawns.

*3* Add the parsley, lemon juice and
seasoning to taste. Pour the sauce
over the fish and eggs and carefully
mix together.

*4* Preheat the oven to 180°C/350°F/
Gas 4. Gently heat the remaining
butter in the remaining milk in a small
saucepan, then beat into the mashed
potato. Spoon evenly over the fish and
fork up the surface.

*5* Sprinkle the cheese over the pie,
then bake for 25–30 minutes,
until golden. Serve piping hot.

# Smoked Trout Pilaff

Smoked trout might seem an unusual partner for rice, but this is a winning combination.

## INGREDIENTS

*Serves 4*

225g / 8oz / 1¼ cups white basmati rice
40g / 1½oz / 3 tbsp butter
2 onions, sliced into rings
1 garlic clove, crushed
2 bay leaves
2 whole cloves
2 green cardamom pods
2 cinnamon sticks
5ml / 1 tsp cumin seeds
4 smoked trout fillets, skinned
50g / 2oz slivered almonds, toasted
50g / 2oz / ⅓ cup seedless raisins
30ml / 2 tbsp chopped fresh parsley
mango chutney and poppadoms,
   to serve

*1* Wash the rice thoroughly in several changes of water and drain well. Set aside. Melt the butter in a large frying pan and fry the onions until well browned, stirring frequently.

*2* Add the garlic, bay leaves, cloves, cardamom pods, cinnamon and cumin seeds and stir-fry for 1 minute.

*3* Stir in the rice, then add 600ml/ 1 pint / 2½ cups boiling water. Bring to the boil. Cover the pan tightly, reduce the heat and cook very gently for 20–25 minutes, until the water has been absorbed and the rice is tender.

*4* Flake the smoked trout and add to the pan with the almonds and raisins. Fork through gently. Re-cover the pan and allow the smoked trout to warm in the rice for a few minutes. Scatter over the parsley and serve with mango chutney and poppadoms.

# Cod with Spiced Red Lentils

## INGREDIENTS

*Serves 4*

175g / 6oz / 1 cup red lentils
1.25ml / ¼ tsp ground turmeric
600ml / 1 pint / 2½ cups fish stock
30ml / 2 tbsp vegetable oil
7.5ml / 1½ tsp cumin seeds
15ml / 1 tbsp grated fresh root ginger
2.5ml / ½ tsp cayenne pepper
15ml / 1 tbsp lemon juice
60ml / 4 tbsp chopped fresh coriander
450g / 1lb cod fillets, skinned and cut
  into large chunks
salt, to taste
coriander sprigs and lemon wedges,
  to garnish

*1* Put the lentils in a pan with the turmeric and stock. Bring to the boil, cover and simmer for 20–25 minutes until the lentils are just tender. Remove from the heat and add salt.

*2* Heat the oil in a small frying pan. Add the cumin seeds and when they begin to pop add the ginger and cayenne pepper. Stir-fry the spices for a few seconds, then pour on to the lentils. Add the lemon juice and 30ml / 2 tbsp of the coriander and stir in gently.

*3* Lay the pieces of cod on top of the lentils, cover the pan and cook gently over a low heat for about 10–15 minutes, until the fish is tender.

*4* Transfer the lentils and cod to warmed serving plates. Sprinkle over the remaining chopped coriander and garnish with one or two lemon wedges. Serve hot.

# Herrings in Oatmeal with Mustard Sauce

## INGREDIENTS

### Serves 4

about 15ml / 1 tbsp Dijon mustard
about 7.5ml / 1½ tsp tarragon vinegar
175ml / 6fl oz / ¾ cup thick mayonnaise
4 herrings, about 225g / 8oz each
1 lemon, halved
115g / 4oz / ¾ cup medium oatmeal
salt and black pepper

*1* Beat mustard and vinegar to taste into the mayonnaise. Chill lightly.

*2* Place one fish at a time on a board, cut side down and opened out. Press gently along the backbone with your thumbs. Turn over the fish and carefully lift away the backbone.

*3* Squeeze lemon juice over both sides of the fish, then season with salt and pepper. Fold the fish in half, skin side outwards.

*4* Preheat a grill until fairly hot. Place the oatmeal on a plate, then coat each herring evenly in the oatmeal, pressing it in gently.

*5* Place the herrings on a grill rack and grill the fish for 3–4 minutes on each side, until the skin is golden brown and crisp and the flesh flakes easily. Serve hot with the mustard sauce, served separately.

# Fish and Chips

## INGREDIENTS

### Serves 4

115g / 4oz / 1 cup self-raising flour
150ml / ¼ pint / ⅔ cup water
675g / 1½lb potatoes
675g / 1½lb piece skinned cod fillet,
   cut into four pieces
oil, for deep frying
salt and black pepper
lemon wedges, to serve

*1* Stir the flour and salt together in a bowl, then form a well in the centre. Gradually pour in the water, whisking in the flour to make a smooth batter. Leave for 30 minutes.

*2* Cut the potatoes into strips about 1cm / ½ in wide and 5cm / 2 in long, using a sharp knife. Place the potatoes in a colander and rinse them in cold water, then drain and dry well.

*3* Heat the oil in a deep-fat fryer or large heavy pan to 150°C / 300°F. Using the wire basket, lower the potatoes in batches into the oil and cook for 5–6 minutes, shaking the basket occasionally until the potatoes are soft but not browned. Remove the chips from the oil and drain thoroughly on kitchen paper.

*4* Heat the oil in the fryer to 190°C / 375°F. Season the fish. Stir the batter, then dip the pieces of fish in turn into it, allowing the excess to drain off.

*5* Working in two batches if necessary, lower the fish into the oil and fry for 6–8 minutes, until crisp and brown. Drain the fish on kitchen paper and keep warm.

*6* Add the chips in batches to the oil and cook for 2–3 minutes, until brown and crisp. Keep hot. Sprinkle with salt and serve with the fish, accompanied by lemon wedges.

# Smoked Haddock Lyonnaise

## INGREDIENTS

*Serves 4*

450g/1lb smoked cod or haddock
150ml/¼ pint/⅔ cup milk
2 onions, chopped
15g/½oz/1 tbsp butter
15ml/1 tbsp cornflour
150ml/¼ pint/⅔ cup Greek-style
   yogurt or fromage frais
5ml/1 tsp ground turmeric
5ml/1 tsp paprika
115g/4oz mushrooms, sliced
2 celery sticks, chopped
350g/12oz firm cooked potatoes,
   preferably cold, diced
30ml/2 tbsp olive oil
25–50g/1–2oz/½–1 cup soft white
   breadcrumbs
salt and black pepper

*1* Poach the fish in the milk until just cooked. Remove the fish, reserving the liquid, then flake the fish and discard the skin and bones. Set aside.

*2* Fry half the chopped onion in the butter until translucent. Stir in the cornflour, then gradually blend in the fish cooking liquid and the yogurt and cook until thickened and smooth.

*3* Stir in the turmeric, paprika, mushrooms and celery. Season to taste and add the flaked fish. Spoon into an ovenproof dish. Preheat the oven to 190°C/375°F/Gas 5.

*4* Fry the remaining onion in the oil until translucent, then add the diced potatoes and stir until lightly coated in oil. Sprinkle on the breadcrumbs and seasoning.

*5* Spoon this mixture over the fish and bake for 20–30 minutes, or until the top is nicely crisp and golden.

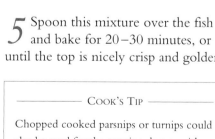

---
COOK'S TIP
---

Chopped cooked parsnips or turnips could also be used for the topping, but as with the potato, it is better if they are firm.

# Golden Fish and Prawn Pie

## INGREDIENTS

*Serves 4–6*

675g / 1½lb white fish fillets
300ml / ½ pint/1¼ cups milk
flavouring ingredients (onion slices,
  bay leaf and black peppercorns)
115g / 4oz cooked, peeled prawns,
  defrosted if frozen
115g / 4oz / ½ cup butter
50g / 2oz / ½ cup plain flour
300ml / ½ pint/1¼ cups single cream
75g / 3oz Gruyère cheese, grated
1 bunch watercress, leaves only, chopped
5ml / 1 tsp Dijon mustard
5 sheets filo pastry
salt and black pepper

*1* Place the fish fillets in a pan, pour over the milk and add the flavouring ingredients. Bring just to the boil, then cover and simmer for 10–12 minutes, until the fish is almost tender.

*2* Skin and bone the fish, then roughly flake into a shallow ovenproof dish. Scatter the prawns over the fish. Strain the milk and reserve.

*3* Melt 50g / 2oz / 4 tbsp of the butter in a pan. Stir in the flour and cook for 1 minute. Stir in the reserved milk and cream. Bring to the boil, stirring, then simmer for 2–3 minutes, until the sauce has thickened.

*4* Remove the pan from the heat and stir in the Gruyère, watercress, mustard and seasoning to taste. Pour over the fish and leave to cool.

*5* Preheat the oven to 190°C/ 375°F/ Gas 5. Melt the remaining butter. Brush one sheet of filo pastry with a little butter, then crumple up loosely and place on top of the filling. Repeat with the remaining filo sheets and butter until they are all used up and the pie is completely covered.

*6* Bake in the oven for 25–30 minutes, until the pastry is golden.

# Herrings with Red Salsa

Herrings are one of the most economical and nutritious fish.
If you buy them ready filleted, they're much easier to eat than the whole fish.

## INGREDIENTS

*Serves 4*
30ml/2 tbsp skimmed milk
10ml/2 tsp Dijon mustard
2 large herrings, filleted
50g/2oz/⅔ cup rolled oats
salt and black pepper

**For the salsa**
1 small red bell pepper, seeded
4 tomatoes
1 spring onion, chopped
15ml/1 tbsp lime juice
5ml/1 tsp caster sugar

*1* Preheat the oven to 200°C/400°F/ Gas 6. To make the salsa, place the pepper, tomatoes, spring onion, lime juice, sugar, and seasoning in a food processor. Process until finely chopped.

*2* Mix the milk and mustard, and the oats and pepper. Dip fillets into the milk mixture, then oats to coat.

*3* Place on a baking sheet and bake for 20 minutes. Serve with the salsa.

> ——— COOK'S TIP ———
>
> If herring fillets are unavailable, then make this recipe with mackerel fillets – they would be equally delicious with the salsa.

# Spiced Rainbow Trout

Farmed rainbow trout are very good value and cook very quickly under a broiler or on a barbecue. Herring and mackerel can be cooked in this way too.

## INGREDIENTS

*Serves 4*
4 large rainbow trout fillets (about 5oz each)
15ml/1 tbsp ground coriander
1 garlic clove, crushed
30ml/2 tbsp finely chopped fresh mint
5ml/1 tsp paprika
175g/6oz/¾ cup natural yogurt
salad and pitta bread, to serve

*1* With a sharp knife, slash the flesh of the fish fillets through the skin fairly deeply at intervals.

*2* Mix together the coriander, garlic, mint, paprika, and yogurt. Spread this mixture evenly over the fish and leave to marinate for about 1 hour.

*3* Cook the fish under a moderately hot grill or on a barbecue, turning occasionally, until crisp and golden. Serve hot, with a crisp salad and some warmed pitta bread.

> ——— COOK'S TIP ———
>
> If you are using the grill, it is best to line the pan with foil before cooking the trout.

> ——— VARIATION ———
>
> The spicy mixture can be used for other fish fillets, such as haddock or cod. Or, use the mixture for kebabs. Coat chunks or strips of fish, then thread on to skewers.

# Spanish Seafood Paella

## INGREDIENTS

### Serves 4

60ml/4 tbsp olive oil
225g/8oz monkfish or cod, skinned
  and cut into chunks
3 prepared baby squid, body cut into
  rings and tentacles chopped
1 red mullet, filleted, skinned and cut
  into chunks (optional)
1 onion, chopped
3 garlic cloves, finely chopped
1 red pepper, seeded and sliced
4 tomatoes, skinned and chopped
225g/8oz/1¼ cups arborio rice
450ml/¾ pint/1⅞ cups fish stock
150ml/¼ pint/⅔ cup white wine
75g/3oz/¾ cup frozen peas
4–5 saffron strands soaked in 30ml/
  2 tbsp hot water
115g/4oz/1 cup cooked, peeled prawns
8 fresh mussels in shells, scrubbed
salt and black pepper
15ml/1 tbsp chopped fresh parsley,
  to garnish
lemon wedges, to serve

*1* Heat 30ml/2 tbsp of the oil in a large frying pan and add the monkfish or cod, the squid and the red mullet, if using, to the pan. Stir-fry for 2 minutes, then transfer the fish to a bowl with all the juices and reserve.

*2* Heat the remaining 30ml/2 tbsp of oil in the pan and add the onion, garlic and pepper. Fry for 6–7 minutes, stirring frequently, until the onions and peppers have softened.

*3* Stir in the tomatoes and fry for 2 minutes, then add the rice, stirring to coat the grains with oil, and cook for 2–3 minutes. Pour on the fish stock and wine and add the peas, saffron and water. Season well and mix.

*4* Gently stir in the reserved cooked fish with all the juices, followed by the prawns and then push the mussels into the rice. Cover and cook over a gentle heat for about 30 minutes, or until the stock has been absorbed but the mixture is still moist.

*5* Remove from the heat, keep covered and leave to stand for 5 minutes. Sprinkle with parsley and serve with lemon wedges.

# Fish Jambalaya

Jambalaya, from New Orleans, is not unlike a paella, but much more spicy. The name comes from the French word jambon, and tells us that the dish is based on ham, but you can add other ingredients of your choice, including all sorts of fish and shellfish.

## INGREDIENTS

*Serves 4*

30ml/2 tbsp oil
115g/4oz smoked bacon, rinds
    removed, diced
1 onion, chopped
2 sticks celery, chopped
2 large garlic cloves, chopped
5ml/1 tsp cayenne pepper
2 bay leaves
5ml/1 tsp dried oregano
2.5ml/½ tsp dried thyme
4 tomatoes, peeled and chopped
150ml/¼ pint/⅔ cup ready-made
    tomato sauce
350g/12oz/1¾ cups long grain rice
475ml/16fl oz/2 cups stock
175g/6oz firm white fish (such as
    coley, cod or haddock), skinned,
    boned and cubed
115g/4oz/1 cup cooked, peeled prawns
salt and black pepper
2 chopped spring onions, to garnish

1 Heat the oil in a large saucepan and fry the bacon until crisp. Add the onion and celery and stir until beginning to stick on the base of the pan.

2 Add the garlic, cayenne pepper, herbs, tomatoes and seasoning and mix well. Stir in the tomato sauce, rice and stock and bring to the boil.

3 Preheat the oven to 180°C/350°F/ Gas 4. Gently stir in the fish and transfer to an ovenproof dish. Cover tightly with foil and bake for 20–30 minutes, until the rice is just tender. Stir in the prawns and heat through. Serve sprinkled with the spring onions.

--- COOK'S TIP ---

A traditional and easy way to serve jambalaya is to fill a 225g/8oz cup with the mixture and unmould it on a hot plate. Then serve with Creole sauce (which you can buy ready-made) and garnish each portion with a whole prawn.

# Seafood Pilaff

This all-in-one-pan main course is a satisfying meal for any day of the week. For a special meal, substitute dry white wine for the orange juice.

**Ingredients** 🍎

*Serves 4*

10ml/2 tsp olive oil
250g/9oz/1¼ cups long-grain rice
5ml/1 tsp ground turmeric
1 red pepper, seeded and diced
1 small onion, finely chopped
2 courgettes, sliced
150g/5oz/2 cups button mushrooms, halved
350ml/12floz/1½ cups fish or chicken broth
150ml/¼ pint/⅔ cup orange juice
350g/12oz white fish fillets
12 cooked, shelled mussels
salt and black pepper
grated rind of 1 orange, to garnish

**1** Heat the oil in a large, non-stick pan and sauté the rice and turmeric over low heat for about 1 minute.

**2** Add the pepper, onion, courgettes, and mushrooms. Stir in the broth and orange juice. Bring to a boil.

**3** Reduce the heat and add the fish. Cover and simmer gently for about 15 minutes, until the rice is tender and the liquid absorbed. Stir in the mussels and heat thoroughly. Adjust the seasoning, sprinkle with orange rind, and serve hot.

--- Cook's tip ---

If you prefer, use fresh mussels in the shell. Scrub well and discard any that remain open. Add 5 minutes before the end of cooking.

# Salmon Pasta with Parsley Sauce

**Ingredients** 🍎

*Serves 4*

450g/1lb salmon fillet, skinned
225g/8oz/3 cups dried pasta, such as penne or twists
175g/6oz cherry tomatoes, halved
150ml/¼ pint/⅔ cup low fat crème fraîche
45ml/3 tbsp chopped fresh parsley
finely grated rind of ½ orange
salt and black pepper

--- Cook's tip ---

If you can't find low fat crème fraîche, then use ordinary crème fraîche or double cream instead.

**1** Cut the salmon into bite-sized pieces, arrange on a heatproof plate, and cover with foil.

**2** Bring a large pan of salted water to the boil, add the pasta, and return to a boil. Place the plate of salmon on top and simmer for 10–12 minutes, until the pasta and salmon are cooked.

**3** Drain the pasta and toss with the tomatoes and salmon. Mix together the crème fraîche, parsley, orange rind, and pepper to taste, then toss into the salmon and pasta and serve hot.

# Baked Fish Creole-style

## INGREDIENTS

*Serves 4*

15ml/1 tbsp olive oil
25g/1oz/2 tbsp butter
1 onion, thinly sliced
1 garlic clove, chopped
1 red pepper, seeded, halved and sliced
1 green pepper, seeded, halved and sliced
400g/14oz can chopped tomatoes with basil
15ml/1 tbsp tomato purée
30ml/2 tbsp capers, chopped
3–4 drops Tabasco sauce
4 tail end pieces cod or haddock fillets (about 175g/6oz each), skinned
6 basil leaves, shredded
45ml/3 tbsp fresh breadcrumbs
25g/1oz/¼ cup grated Cheddar cheese
10ml/2 tsp chopped fresh parsley
salt and black pepper
fresh basil sprigs, to garnish

*1* Preheat the oven to 230°C/450°F/ Gas 8. Butter an ovenproof dish.

*2* Heat the oil and half the butter in a pan and add the onion. Fry for about 6–7 minutes, until softened, then add the garlic, peppers, chopped tomatoes, tomato purée, capers and Tabasco and season well. Cover and cook for 15 minutes, then uncover and simmer gently for 5 minutes to reduce slightly.

*3* Place the fish fillets in the oven-proof dish, dot with the remaining 15g/½oz/1 tbsp butter and season lightly. Spoon over the tomato and pepper sauce and sprinkle over the shredded basil. Bake in the oven for about 10 minutes.

*4* Meanwhile, mix together the bread-crumbs, cheese and parsley in a bowl.

*5* Remove the fish from the oven and scatter the cheese and bread-crumbs over the top. Return to the oven and bake for a further 10 min-utes, until lightly browned.

*6* Let the fish stand for about a minute, then, using a fish slice, carefully transfer each topped fillet to warmed plates. Garnish with sprigs of fresh basil and serve hot.

# Moroccan Fish Tagine

Tagine is actually the name of the large Moroccan pottery dish used for this type of cooking, but you can use an ordinary baking dish instead.

### INGREDIENTS 

*Serves 4*

2 garlic cloves, crushed
30ml/2 tbsp ground cumin
30ml/2 tbsp paprika
1 small fresh red chilli
30ml/2 tbsp tomato purée
60ml/4 tbsp lemon juice
4 whiting or cod steaks, about
   175g/6oz each
350g/12oz tomatoes, sliced
2 green bell peppers, seeded and
   thinly sliced
salt and black pepper
chopped fresh coriander, to garnish

*1* Mix together the garlic, cumin, paprika, chilli, tomato purée and lemon juice. Spread this mixture over the fish, then cover and chill for about 30 minutes to let the flavour penetrate.

*2* Preheat the oven to 200°C/400°F/ Gas 6. Arrange half of the tomatoes and peppers in a baking dish.

*3* Cover with the fish, in one layer, then arrange the remaining tomatoes and pepper on top. Cover the baking dish with foil and bake for about 45 minutes, until the fish is cooked through. Sprinkle with chopped coriander and serve.

---

#### COOK'S TIP

If you are preparing this dish for a dinner party, it can be assembled completely and stored in the fridge, ready for baking when needed.

---

#### VARIATION

For a colourful variation, replace one of the green peppers with a yellow or orange pepper. You could use chopped parsley, if you can't find fresh coriander.

# Crunchy-topped Cod

Delicious and quick to cook, this is ideal for weekday meals.

**INGREDIENTS** 🍎

*Serves 4*

4 pieces cod fillet, about 115g/4oz
    each, skinned
2 medium tomatoes, sliced
1 cup fresh wholemeal breadcrumbs
30ml/2 tbsp chopped fresh parsley
finely grated rind and juice of ½ lemon
5ml/1tsp sunflower oil
salt and black pepper

*1* Preheat the oven to 200°C/400°F/
Gas 6. Arrange the cod fillets in a
wide, ovenproof dish.

*2* Arrange the tomato slices on top.
Mix together the breadcrumbs,
fresh parsley, lemon rind and juice, and
the oil with seasoning to taste.

*3* Spoon the crumb mixture evenly
over the fish, then bake for 15–20
minutes. Serve hot.

———— COOK'S TIP ————

Choose firm, ripe tomatoes with plenty of
flavour. In the summer you may be lucky
enough to find fresh plum tomatoes,
which are perfect for this tasty dish.

# Crumbly Fish Bake

This fish pie is colourful, healthy,
and best of all very easy to make.
For a more economical version,
omit the prawns and replace with
more fish fillet.

**INGREDIENTS** 🍎

*Serves 4*

350g/12oz haddock fillet, skinned
30ml/2 tbsp cornflour
115g/4oz cooked, peeled prawns
200g/7oz can sweetcorn, drained
75g/3oz/¾ cup frozen peas
150ml/¼ pint/⅔ cup skimmed milk
150g/5oz/⅔ cup low fat fromage frais
75g/3oz/1½ cups fresh wholemeal
    breadcrumbs
40g/1½ oz/½ cup grated low fat
    Cheddar cheese
salt and black pepper

*1* Preheat the oven to 190°C/375°F/
Gas 5. Cut the haddock into bite-
sized pieces and toss in cornflour.

*2* Place the fish, shrimp, corn, and
peas in an ovenproof dish. Beat
together the milk, fromage frais, and
seasonings, then pour into the dish.

*3* Mix together the breadcrumbs and
grated cheese, then spoon evenly
over the top. Bake for 25–30 minutes,
or until golden brown. Serve hot, with
fresh vegetables.

———— COOK'S TIP ————

This quick recipe can be prepared well
ahead and chilled – keep the breadcrumb
topping separately, then sprinkle over the
fish mixture just before baking.

# Cod Creole

**Serves 4**
450g/1lb cod fillets, skinned
15ml/1 tbsp lime or lemon juice
10ml/2 tsp olive oil
1 medium onion, finely chopped
1 green pepper, seeded and sliced
2.5ml/½ tsp cayenne pepper
2.5ml/½ tsp garlic salt
400g/14oz can chopped tomatoes

---
COOK'S TIP

Be careful not to overcook the fish – or to
let it bubble too vigorously in the sauce –
as the chunks will break up.

---

*1* Cut the cod fillets into bite-sized
chunks and sprinkle with the lime
or lemon juice.

*2* In a large, non-stick pan, heat the
olive oil and sauté the onion and
pepper gently until softened. Add the
cayenne pepper and garlic salt.

*3* Stir in the cod with the chopped
tomatoes. Bring to a boil, then
cover and simmer for about 5 minutes,
or until the fish flakes easily. Serve
with boiled rice or potatoes.

# Five-spice Fish

Chinese mixtures of spicy, sweet,
and sour flavours are particularly
successful with fish – and dinner is
ready in minutes!

**Serves 4**
4 white fish fillets, such as cod, haddock
  or hoki (about 175g/6oz each)
5ml/1 tsp Chinese five-spice powder
20ml/4 tsp cornflour
15ml/1 tbsp sesame or sunflower oil
3 spring onions, shredded
5ml/1 tsp finely chopped root ginger
150g/5oz button mushrooms, sliced
115g/4oz baby corn, sliced
30ml/2 tbsp soy sauce
45ml/3 tbsp dry sherry or apple juice
5ml/1 tsp sugar
salt and black pepper

*1* Toss the fish in the five-spice
powder and cornflour to coat.

*2* Heat the oil in a frying pan or wok
and stir-fry the spring onions,
ginger, mushrooms, and corn for about
1 minute. Add the fish and cook for
2–3 minutes, turning once.

*3* Mix together the soy sauce, sherry,
and sugar, then pour over the fish.
Simmer for 2 minutes, adjust the
seasoning, then serve with noodles and
stir-fried vegetables.

---
COOK'S TIP

Chinese noodles are available in most large
supermarkets and make a very speedy
accompaniment since they are just soaked
in boiling water for a few minutes.

---

# DINNER PARTY DISHES

The perfect food for entertaining is easy to prepare and serve, yet looks
fabulous and tastes wonderful. Fish makes an especially good choice for
a main course, as it is not too rich, yet is full of flavour. If you prefer to
have the main dish prepared ahead of time try Monkfish Brochettes.
However, if you don't mind cooking at the last minute, then Tuna
with Pan-fried Tomatoes or flash-fried salmon are perfect choices.

# Halibut with Fennel and Orange

## INGREDIENTS

*Serves 4*

1 fennel bulb, thinly sliced
grated rind and juice of 1 orange
150ml/¼ pint/⅔ cup dry white wine
4 halibut steaks, about 200g/7oz each
50g/2oz/4 tbsp butter
salt and black pepper
fennel fronds, to garnish

*1* Preheat the oven to 180°C/350°F/
Gas 4. Butter a shallow baking dish.

*2* Add the fennel to a saucepan of
boiling water, return to the boil
and boil for 4–6 minutes, until just
tender.

*3* Meanwhile, cook the orange rind,
juice and wine until reduced by half.

*4* Drain the fennel well, then spread
in the baking dish and season.
Arrange the halibut on the fennel,
season, dot with butter, then pour
over the reduced orange and wine.

*5* Cover and bake for about 20
minutes, until the flesh flakes.
Serve garnished with fennel fronds.

# Salmon with Cucumber Sauce

## INGREDIENTS

*Serves 6–8*

1.8kg/4lb salmon, gutted
  and scaled
melted butter, for brushing
3 parsley or thyme sprigs
½ lemon, halved
1 large cucumber, peeled
25g/1oz/2 tbsp butter
115ml/4fl oz/½ cup dry white wine
45ml/3 tbsp finely chopped fresh dill
60ml/4 tbsp soured cream
salt and black pepper

*1* Preheat the oven to 220°C/425°F/
Gas 7. Season the salmon and brush
inside and out with melted butter.
Place the herbs and lemon in the cavity.

*2* Wrap the salmon in foil, folding the
edges together securely, then bake
for 15 minutes. Remove the fish from
the oven and leave in the foil for 1 hour,
then remove the skin from the salmon.

*3* Meanwhile, halve the cucumber
lengthways, scoop out the seeds,
then dice the flesh.

*4* Place the cucumber in a colander,
toss lightly with salt, leave for
about 30 minutes to drain, then rinse
well and pat dry.

*5* Heat the butter in a small saucepan,
add the cucumber and cook for
about 2 minutes, until translucent but
not soft. Add the wine to the pan and
boil briskly until the cucumber is dry.

*6* Stir the chopped dill and soured
cream into the cooked cucumber.
Season to taste and serve immediately
with the salmon.

# Mediterranean Plaice Rolls

Sun-dried tomatoes, toasted pine nuts and anchovies make a flavoursome combination for the stuffing mixture.

### INGREDIENTS

*Serves 4*

4 plaice fillets, about 225g/8oz each, skinned
75g/3oz/6 tbsp butter
1 small onion, chopped
1 celery stick, finely chopped
115g/4oz/2 cups fresh white bread-crumbs
45ml/3 tbsp chopped fresh parsley
30ml/2 tbsp pine nuts, toasted
3–4 pieces sun-dried tomatoes in oil, drained and chopped
50g/2oz can anchovy fillets, drained and chopped
75ml/5 tbsp fish stock
black pepper

1 Preheat the oven to 180°C/350°F/ Gas 4. Using a sharp knife, cut the plaice fillets in half lengthways to make eight smaller fillets.

2 Melt the butter in a pan and add the onion and celery. Cover and cook over a low heat for about 15 minutes until softened. Do not allow to brown.

3 Mix together the breadcrumbs, parsley, pine nuts, sun-dried toma-toes and anchovies. Stir in the softened vegetables with the buttery juices and season with pepper.

4 Divide the stuffing into eight portions. Taking one portion at a time, form the stuffing into balls, then roll up each one inside a plaice fillet. Secure each roll with a cocktail stick.

5 Place the rolled-up fillets in a buttered ovenproof dish. Pour in the stock and cover the dish with buttered foil. Bake for about 20 minutes, or until the fish flakes easily. Remove the cocktail sticks, then serve with a little of the cooking juices drizzled over.

# Red Mullet with Fennel

Ask the fishmonger to gut the mullet but not to discard the liver, as this is a delicacy and provides much of the flavour.

## INGREDIENTS

*Serves 4*

3 small fennel bulbs
60ml / 4 tbsp olive oil
2 small onions, thinly sliced
4 basil leaves
4 small or 2 large red mullet, cleaned
grated rind of ½ lemon
150ml / ¼ pint / ⅔ cup fish stock
50g / 2oz / 4 tbsp butter
juice of 1 lemon

*1* Snip off the feathery fronds from the fennel, finely chop and reserve for the garnish. Cut the fennel into wedges, leaving the layers attached at the root ends so the pieces stay intact.

*2* Heat the oil in a frying pan large enough to take the fish in a single layer. Add the wedges of fennel and the onions and cook for 10–15 minutes, until softened and lightly browned.

*3* Tuck a basil leaf inside each mullet, then place on top of the vegetables. Sprinkle over the lemon rind. Pour in the stock and bring just to the boil. Cover and cook gently for 15–20 minutes, until the fish is tender.

*4* Melt the remaining butter in a pan and when it starts to sizzle and colour slightly, add the lemon juice. Pour over the mullet, sprinkle with the reserved fennel fronds and serve.

# Baked Trout with Olives

## INGREDIENTS

*Serves 4*

50g/2oz/1 cup fresh wholemeal
  breadcrumbs
25g/1oz chopped ham
50g/2oz/½ cup finely chopped black
  olives
1 garlic clove, crushed
1 egg yolk
4 trout (about 175g/6oz each)
120ml/4fl oz/¼ cup dry martini
25g/1oz/2 tbsp butter
15g/½oz/1 tbsp plain flour
150ml/¼ pint/⅔ cup fish stock
45–60ml/3–4 tbsp single cream
salt and black pepper

*1* Preheat the oven to 180°C/350°F/
Gas 4. Mix the breadcrumbs, ham,
olives, garlic, egg yolk and seasoning
together. Pack into the trout and place
each one on a sheet of greased foil.

*2* Pour 15ml/1 tbsp dry martini over
each one, dot with half of the butter and wrap up closely. Bake for
20–25 minutes, or until tender.

*3* Melt the remaining butter in a
small pan and blend in the flour.
Whisk in the remaining martini, the
stock and the juices which have come
out of the fish during cooking and
cook for 1–2 minutes until thickened.

*4* Stir in the cream, then season the
sauce to taste and pour a little over
each fish before serving hot.

# Salmon Cakes with Butter Sauce

Salmon fish cakes make a real treat
for an informal dinner party. You
could use any small tail pieces
which are on special offer.

## INGREDIENTS

*Makes 6*

225g/8oz tail piece of salmon, cooked
30ml/2 tbsp chopped fresh parsley
2 spring onions, trimmed and chopped
grated rind and juice of ½ lemon
225g/8oz cooked mashed potato
1 egg, beaten
50g/2oz/1 cup fresh white breadcrumbs
75g/3oz/6 tbsp butter
salt and black pepper

*1* Remove all the skin and bones
from the fish and flake it well. Add
the parsley, onions, 5ml/1 tsp of the
lemon rind and seasoning.

*2* Gently work in the potato and then
shape into six rounds, triangles or
croquettes. Chill for 20 minutes.

*3* Coat well in egg and then the
bread-crumbs. Grill gently for 5
minutes each side, or until golden, or
fry in a little butter and oil.

*4* To make the butter sauce, melt the
butter, whisk in the remaining
lemon rind, the lemon juice, 15–30ml/
1–2 tbsp water and seasoning to taste.
Simmer for a few minutes and serve
with the hot fish cakes.

# Cod with Caper Sauce

The quick and easy sauce with a slightly sharp and 'nutty' flavour is a very effective way of enhancing this simple fish.

## INGREDIENTS

### Serves 4

4 cod steaks, about 175g/6oz each
115g/4oz/ ½ cup butter
15ml/1 tbsp vinegar from the caper jar
15ml/1 tbsp small capers
15ml/1 tbsp chopped fresh parsley
salt and black pepper
tarragon sprigs, to garnish

1 Preheat the grill. Season the cod. Melt 25g/1oz/2 tbsp of the butter, then brush some over one side of each piece of cod.

2 Grill the cod steaks for about 6 minutes, turn the fish over, then brush with melted butter and cook for a further 5–6 minutes, or until the fish flakes easily.

3 Meanwhile, heat the remaining butter until it turns golden brown, then add the vinegar followed by the capers and stir well.

4 Pour the vinegar, butter and capers over the fish, sprinkle with parsley and garnish with the tarragon sprigs.

---

COOK'S TIP

Thick tail fillets of cod or haddock could be used in place of the cod steaks.

---

# Trout with Hazelnuts

The shelled hazelnuts in this recipe make an interesting change from the flaked almonds normally used with trout.

## INGREDIENTS

*Serves 4*
50g/2oz/⅓ cup shelled hazelnuts, chopped
65g/2½oz/5 tbsp butter
4 trout, about 275g/10oz each
30ml/2 tbsp lemon juice
salt and black pepper
lemon slices and flat leaf parsley sprigs, to serve

*1* Preheat the grill. Toast the hazelnuts in a single layer, stirring frequently, until the skins split. Then tip them on to a clean tea towel and rub to remove the skins. Leave the hazelnuts to cool, then chop them coarsely.

*2* Heat 50g/2oz/4 tbsp of the butter in a large frying pan. Season the trout inside and out, then fry two at a time for 12–15 minutes, turning once, until the trout are brown and the flesh flakes easily when tested with the point of a sharp knife.

*3* Drain the cooked trout on kitchen paper, then transfer to a warm serving plate and keep warm while frying the remaining trout in the same way. (If your frying pan is large enough, you could, of course, cook the trout in one batch.)

*4* Add the remaining butter to the frying pan, then add the hazelnuts and fry them until evenly browned. Stir the lemon juice into the pan and mix well, then quickly pour the buttery sauce over the trout and serve at once, garnished with slices of lemon and flat leaf parsley sprigs.

---
— COOK'S TIP —

You can use a microwave to prepare the nuts, spread them in a shallow dish and cook on full power until the skins split.

# Plaice and Pesto Parcels

Serve the parcels hot from the oven to the table – the paper bakes translucent and looks attractive.

**INGREDIENTS**

*Serves 4*
75g / 3oz / 6 tbsp butter
20ml / 4 tsp pesto sauce
8 small plaice fillets
1 small fennel bulb, cut into
 matchsticks
2 small carrots, cut into matchsticks
2 courgettes, cut into matchsticks
10ml / 2 tsp finely grated lemon rind
salt and black pepper
basil leaves, to garnish

*1* Preheat the oven to 190°C / 375°F/ Gas 5. Beat 50g/2oz /4 tbsp of the butter with the pesto and seasoning to taste. Skin the plaice fillets, then spread the pesto butter over the skinned side of each and roll up, starting from the thick end. Set the plaice rolls aside.

*2* Melt the remaining butter in a pan, add the fennel and carrots and sauté for 3 minutes. Add the courgettes and cook for 2 minutes. Remove from the heat. Add the lemon rind and seasoning.

*3* Cut four squares of greaseproof paper, each large enough to enclose two plaice rolls. Brush with oil. Spoon the vegetables into the centre of each, then place two plaice rolls on top.

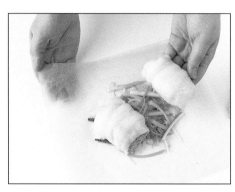

*4* Seal the parcels tightly and place in a roasting tin. Bake for 15–20 minutes, until the fish is just tender.

*5* To serve, open up the parcels, then sprinkle with the basil leaves and grind over a little black pepper.

# Skate with Lemon and Capers

Skate wings served with a sharp, herby sauce make a different – and very easy – main course.

**INGREDIENTS**

*Serves 4*
4 small skate wings, about
 175–225g / 6–8oz each
seasoned plain flour
90ml / 6 tbsp olive oil
1 garlic clove, crushed
finely grated rind of ½ lemon
juice of 1 large lemon
30ml / 2 tbsp capers, rinsed, drained
 and chopped
30ml / 2 tbsp chopped fresh flat leaf
 parsley
15ml / 1 tbsp chopped fresh basil
15ml / 1 tbsp snipped fresh chives
salt and black pepper

*1* Lightly dust the skate wings in the seasoned flour. Heat 30ml / 2 tbsp of the oil in a large frying pan and, when hot, add the skate wings and fry for 8–10 minutes, turning once, until the flesh begins to part easily from the bone and looks creamy white.

*2* Meanwhile, mix together the remaining oil, the garlic, lemon rind and juice in a bowl with the capers, parsley, basil, chives and seasoning.

*3* Pour the sauce into the pan to warm it through. Transfer the skate to warmed serving plates and serve with the sauce spooned on top.

# Spanish-style Hake

Cod and haddock cutlets will work just as well as hake in this tasty fish dish.

**INGREDIENTS**

*Serves 4*
30ml / 2 tbsp olive oil
25g / 1oz / 2 tbsp butter
1 onion, chopped
3 garlic cloves, crushed
15ml / 1 tbsp plain flour
2.5ml / ½ tsp paprika
4 hake cutlets, about 175g / 6oz each
250g / 8oz fine green beans, cut into
    2.5cm / 1in lengths
350ml / 12fl oz / 1½ cups fresh fish stock
150ml / ¼ pint / ⅔ cup dry white wine
30ml / 2 tbsp dry sherry
16–20 live mussels, cleaned
45ml / 3 tbsp chopped fresh parsley
salt and black pepper
crusty bread, to serve

*1* Heat the oil and butter in a sauté or frying pan, add the onion and cook for 5 minutes, until softened, but not browned. Add the crushed garlic and cook for 1 minute more.

*2* Mix together the plain flour and paprika, then lightly dust over the hake cutlets. Push the onion and garlic to one side of the pan.

*3* Add the hake cutlets to the pan and fry until golden on both sides. Stir in the beans, stock, wine, sherry and seasoning. Bring to the boil and cook for about 2 minutes.

*4* Add the mussels and parsley, cover the pan and cook for 5–8 minutes, until the mussels have opened.

*5* Serve the hake in warmed, shallow soup bowls with crusty bread to mop up the juices.

# Monkfish with Mexican Salsa

## INGREDIENTS

*Serves 4*
675g / 1½lb monkfish tail
45ml / 3 tbsp olive oil
30ml / 2 tbsp lime juice
1 garlic clove, crushed
15ml / 1 tbsp chopped fresh coriander
salt and black pepper
coriander sprigs and lime slices,
 to garnish

**For the salsa**
4 tomatoes, peeled, seeded and diced
1 avocado, peeled, stoned and diced
½ red onion, chopped
1 green chilli, seeded and chopped
30ml / 2 tbsp chopped fresh coriander
30ml / 2 tbsp olive oil
15ml / 1 tbsp lime juice

*1* To make the salsa, mix the salsa ingredients and leave at room temperature for about 30 minutes.

*2* Prepare the monkfish. Using a sharp knife, remove the pinkish-grey membrane. Cut the fillets from either side of the backbone, then cut each fillet in half to give four steaks.

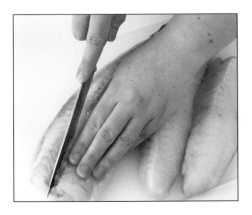

*3* Mix together the oil, lime juice, garlic, coriander and seasoning in a shallow non-metallic dish. Add the monkfish steaks to the dish. Turn the monkfish several times to coat with the marinade, then cover the dish and leave to marinate at cool room temperature, or in the fridge, for several hours.

*4* Remove the monkfish from the marinade and grill for 10–12 minutes, turning once and brushing regularly with the marinade until cooked through.

*5* Serve the monkfish garnished with coriander sprigs and lime slices and accompanied by the salsa.

— COOK'S TIP —

It is important to remove the tough pinkish-grey membrane covering the monkfish tail before cooking, otherwise it will shrink and toughen the monkfish.

# Tuna with Pan-fried Tomatoes

### INGREDIENTS

*Serves 2*

2 tuna steaks, about 175g/6oz each
90ml/6 tbsp olive oil
30ml/2 tbsp lemon juice
2 garlic cloves, chopped
5ml/1 tsp chopped fresh thyme
4 canned anchovy fillets, drained and
   finely chopped
225g/8oz plum tomatoes, halved
30ml/2 tbsp chopped fresh parsley
4–6 black olives, pitted and chopped
black pepper
crusty bread, to serve

---

—————— COOK'S TIP ——————

If you are unable to find fresh tuna steaks,
you could replace them with salmon fillets, if you like – just cook them for one
or two minutes more on each side.

---

1 Place the tuna steaks in a shallow non-metallic dish. Mix 60ml/4 tbsp of the oil with the lemon juice, garlic, thyme, anchovies and pepper. Pour this mixture over the tuna and leave to marinate for at least 1 hour.

2 Lift the tuna from the marinade and place on a grill rack. Grill for 4 minutes on each side, or until the tuna feels firm to touch, basting with the marinade. Take care not to overcook.

3 Meanwhile, heat the remaining oil in a frying pan. Add the tomatoes and fry for 1 minute only on each side.

4 Divide the tomatoes equally between two serving plates and scatter over the chopped parsley and olives. Top each with a tuna steak.

5 Add the remaining marinade to the pan juices and warm through. Pour over the tomatoes and tuna steaks and serve at once with crusty bread for mopping up the juices.

# Scottish Salmon with Herb Butter

### INGREDIENTS

*Serves 4*

50g/2oz/4 tbsp butter, softened
finely grated rind of ½ small lemon
15ml/1 tbsp lemon juice
15ml/1 tbsp chopped fresh dill
4 salmon steaks
2 lemon slices, halved
4 fresh dill sprigs
salt and black pepper

*1* Place the butter, lemon rind, lemon juice, chopped dill and seasoning in a small bowl and mix together with a fork until blended.

*2* Spoon the butter on to a piece of greaseproof paper and roll up, smoothing with your hands into a sausage shape. Twist the ends tightly, wrap in clear film and pop in the freezer for 20 minutes, until firm.

*3* Meanwhile, preheat the oven to 190°C/375°F/Gas 5. Cut out four squares of foil big enough to encase the salmon steaks and grease lightly. Place a salmon steak in the centre of each one.

*4* Remove the butter from the freezer and slice into eight rounds. Place two rounds on top of each salmon steak with a halved lemon slice in the centre and a sprig of dill on top. Lift up the edges of the foil and crinkle them together until well sealed.

*5* Lift the parcels on to a baking sheet and bake for about 20 minutes. Remove from the oven and place the unopened parcels on warmed plates. Open the parcels and slide the contents on to the plates with the juices.

---

### COOK'S TIP

Other fresh herbs could be used to flavour the butter – try chopped mint, fennel fronds, lemon balm, parsley or oregano instead of the dill.

# Chargrilled Squid

## INGREDIENTS

### Serves 4

1kg / 2lb prepared squid
90ml / 6 tbsp olive oil
juice of 1–2 lemons
3 garlic cloves, crushed
1.25ml / ¼ tsp hot red pepper flakes
60ml / 4 tbsp chopped fresh parsley
lemon wedges, to garnish

*1* Reserve the squid tentacles, then using a small sharp knife, score the flesh into a diagonal pattern.

*2* Place all the squid in a shallow non-metallic dish. To make the marinade, mix together the olive oil, lemon juice, crushed garlic and hot red pepper flakes in a small bowl.

*3* Pour the marinade over the squid and leave in a cool place for at least 2 hours, stirring occasionally.

*4* Lift the squid from the marinade and barbecue for 2 minutes on each side, turning them frequently and brushing with the marinade until the outside is golden brown and crisp, with soft, moist flesh inside.

*5* Bring the remaining marinade to the boil in a small pan, stir in the chopped parsley, then pour over the squid. Garnish with lemon wedges and serve at once.

---
COOK'S TIP

If you are in a rush, it is still worth marinating the squid – even for 20 minutes – as this will both tenderize and flavour it.

---

# Monkfish Brochettes

## INGREDIENTS

### Serves 4

675g / 1½lb monkfish, skinned and boned
12 rashers streaky bacon, rinded
2 small courgettes
1 yellow or orange pepper, seeded and cut into 2.5cm / 1in cubes

### For the marinade

90ml / 6 tbsp olive oil
grated rind of ½ lime
45ml / 3 tbsp lime juice
30ml / 2 tbsp dry white wine
60ml / 4 tbsp chopped fresh mixed herbs, such as dill, chives and parsley
5ml / 1 tsp clear honey
black pepper
saffron rice and green salad, to serve
fresh herb sprigs and lime wedges, to garnish

*1* To make the marinade, mix together the olive oil, lime rind and juice, wine, chopped herbs, honey and pepper in a bowl, then set aside.

*2* Cut the monkfish into 24 x 2.5cm / 1in cubes. Stretch the bacon rashers with the back of a knife, then cut each piece in half and wrap around the monkfish cubes.

*3* Pare strips of peel from the courgettes to give a stripy effect, then cut into 2.5cm / 1in chunks.

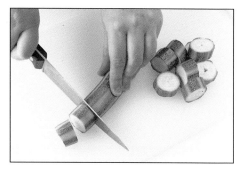

*4* Thread the fish rolls on to skewers alternately with the courgettes and pepper. Place in a dish. Pour over the marinade and leave in a cool place for 1 hour. Lift out the skewers, then grill for about 10 minutes, turning and basting occasionally with the marinade. Serve with saffron rice and a green salad. Garnish with herbs and lime.

# Flash-fried Salmon with Mint Salsa

A little piece of salmon treated like this can go a surprisingly long way, with little or no effort. It is good with cod, too.

**INGREDIENTS**

*Serves 4*

2 large extra tasty tomatoes, peeled, seeded and diced
7.5cm/3in piece of cucumber, peeled and diced
5ml/1 tsp balsamic or red wine vinegar
30ml/2 tbsp chopped fresh mint, or 10ml/2 tsp dried
45ml/3 tbsp olive oil
4 salmon tail fillet pieces (about 450g/ 1lb weight), or 1 tail piece which you will need to fillet yourself
25g/1oz/2 tbsp butter
squeeze of lemon juice
salt and black pepper

*1* To make the salsa, mix the diced tomatoes, cucumber, vinegar, mint and 15–30ml/1–2 tbsp olive oil together and season to taste. Chill.

*2* Lay the fish between sheets of greaseproof paper and gently bash with a rolling pin, to make them as flat as possible. Brush both sides with oil and season with salt and black pepper.

*3* Heat half the butter in a non-stick frying pan and, when really hot, fry the fillets two at a time. Allow only about 1 minute each side and serve at once with a squeeze of lemon juice and the chilled salsa.

# Roast Cod with Mixed Beans

**INGREDIENTS**

*Serves 4*

4 thick cod steaks
45ml/3 tbsp sweet sherry or Madeira
400g/14oz can spicy mixed beans, drained
400g/14oz kidney, borlotti or flageolet beans, drained
2 garlic cloves, crushed
15ml/1 tbsp olive oil
5ml/1 tsp grated orange rind
15ml/1 tbsp chopped fresh parsley
salt and black pepper

*1* Skin the steaks, then pour over the sherry or Madeira and leave in a bowl, turning once, for 10 minutes.

*2* Preheat the oven to 200°C/400°F/ Gas 6. Mix the beans with the garlic and place in the base of an ovenproof dish. Place the fish on top and pour over the sherry or Madeira. Brush the fish with the oil, sprinkle with orange rind, half the parsley and seasoning.

*3* Cover tightly with foil and cook for 15–20 minutes. Pierce the thickest part of the fish with a knife to check if it is cooked through and continue cooking for only another 2–3 minutes if necessary.

*4* Baste the fish with a little of the juices which will have risen to the top of the beans. Then sprinkle with the rest of the parsley just before serving.

# INDEX